what about...
science &
technology?

what about...
science &
technology?

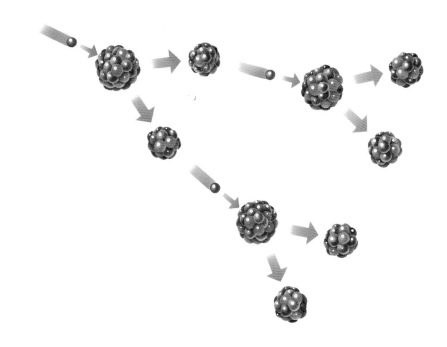

Steve Parker

Miles Kelly
PUBLISHING

First published in 2004 by Miles Kelly Publishing Ltd
Harding's Barn, Bardfield End Green, Thaxted, Essex, CM6 3PX

This edition printed in 2011 by Miles Kelly Publishing Ltd

4 6 8 10 9 7 5

British Library Cataloguing-in-Publication Data
A catalogue record for this book is available from the British Library

ISBN 978-1-84236-793-3

Printed in China

Editorial Director Belinda Gallagher
Art Director Jo Brewer
Senior Editor Jenni Rainford
Assistant Editors Lucy Dowling, Teri Mort
Copy Editor Rosalind Beckman
Design Concept John Christopher
Volume Designers Jo Brewer, Michelle Cannatella
Picture Researcher Liberty Newton
Indexer Helen Snaith
Production Manager Elizabeth Collins
Reprographics Anthony Cambray, Stephan Davis, Liberty Newton, Ian Paulyn

www.mileskelly.net
info@mileskelly.net

www.factsforprojects.com

CONTENTS

The Basics of Matter 8–9

What are substances made of?
Are atoms the smallest pieces of matter?
What are quarks?
What holds the parts of an atom together?
Are all atoms the same?

Chemicals and Compounds 10–11

Do atoms join together?
Are atoms ever alone?
How else do atoms join?
What is a compound?
How many atoms are in a compound?

Structures and Materials 12–13

How is a material's strength measured?
What are other features of materials?
What are natural materials?
What material is most commonly used?
Is a tin can really made of tin?

Energy and Work 14–15

Where is energy?
Can energy be made or destroyed?
What happens in an energy chain?
Can energy be created from atoms?
What is nuclear energy?

Electricity and Power 16–17

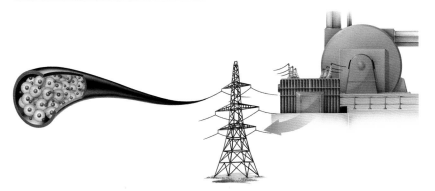

What is electricity?
Do all substances carry electricity?
How do batteries work?
What happens inside a power station?
What are DC and AC?

6 CONTENTS

Magnetism 18–19

What is a magnet?
How is magnetism made?
Which substances are magnetic?
Can magnets be switched on and off?
Are magnets common?
How does an electric motor work?

The Electronic Age 20–21

How do electronic devices work?
Do electronic devices use much electricity?
What are ICs?
What is a microchip?
What are CPUs?

Rays and Radiation 22–23

What is radiation?
Can radiation be emitted as particles, not waves?
Is 'radioactivity' radiation?
How fast does radiation travel?
Is radiation harmful?

Light and Lasers 24–25

What is light?
Is light always in the form of waves?
Why are there different colours of light?
Does light always travel in straight lines?
How fast is light?

Sound 26–27

What is sound?
Can we see sounds?
Can we hear all sounds?
How fast does sound travel?
Can sound reflect, like light?

Force, Motion and Machines 28–29

What is a force?
  Do atoms move?
    Are there different kinds of motion?
      What is a machine?
        Do machines give us extra energy?

Time and Space 30–31

When did people start measuring time?
When were clocks first developed?
Could time stand still?
Is it the same time everywhere in the world?
Are time and space linked?

Transport and Communications 32–33

Is the world really 'shrinking'?
  Will travel times continue to shorten?
    What is a comsat?
      What are the fastest forms of transport?
    Which form of travel is most luxurious?
  Will we have personal jump-jets or helicopters?

Technology Today and Tomorrow 34–35

How do CDs and DVDs store information?
Which labour-saving devices are most popular?
Can mobile phones get much smaller?
Does medicine benefit from technology?
How fast does technology become out-of-date?

Quiz Time   36–37

Index   38–40

Matter is anything and everything in the Universe. It includes all substances, items and objects, whether solid, liquid or gas – and not only here on Earth, but deep into space, to the Sun and beyond, in fact, all through the entire Universe. So there is plenty of matter! Studying what it is made of is one of the great quests of modern science.

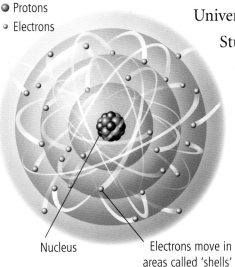

- Neutrons
- Protons
- Electrons

Nucleus

Electrons move in areas called 'shells'

➊ *Uranium is a very hard, heavy metal. Its atoms, such as this one above, are among the largest of all atoms, with 92 protons and about 146 neutrons in the nucleus, and 92 electrons to balance the protons.*

What are substances made of?

All substances consist of atoms. If you could chop up any substance smaller and smaller, the pieces would become too small to see. But if you could keep chopping, under the most powerful microscope, eventually you would reach the tiniest pieces or atoms of the substance. All matter is made of atoms.

Are atoms the smallest pieces of matter?

No, each atom is made up of even smaller parts, known as subatomic particles. There are three kinds of subatomic particles– protons, neutrons and electrons. Protons and neutrons clump together at the centre of the atom, called the nucleus. Electrons whizz round and round the nucleus. If an atom is split, it no longer has the features of the original substance.

➋ *The simplest and lightest atom of all is hydrogen. It has just one proton as the nucleus and one electron going around it. Helium is next, with a nucleus of two protons and two neutrons, and two orbiting electrons. Oxygen is more complex, with eight of each particle – protons, neutrons and electrons.*

What are quarks?

Some scientists believe that subatomic particles are made of even tinier pieces of matter known as quarks. For example, a proton is composed of three quarks. Other scientists believe that atoms, quarks and all other matter are made of far smaller vibrating lengths of energy called 'strings'. If an atom was the size of planet Earth, a 'string' would be the size of a shoelace. These 'strings' may join into 'superstrings' that could even stretch past lots of atoms. Scientists are beginning to investigate whether 'strings' really exist.

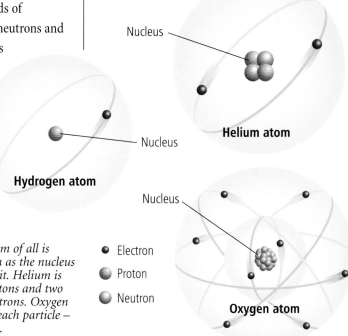

Nucleus

Nucleus

Helium atom

Nucleus

Hydrogen atom

- Electron
- Proton
- Neutron

Oxygen atom

Atomic facts

Key dates

2500 BC Empedocles from ancient Greece suggested that all matter was made of mixtures of four elements – earth, air, fire and water.

2400 BC Greek philosopher, Democritus, developed the idea that matter could be cut so small that it could not be cut any more. He named these pieces of matter 'atoms', meaning 'uncuttable'.

340 BC Greek thinker and scientist Aristotle added ether to the elements.

1661 English scientist Robert Boyle described elements as "simple or perfectly unmingled bodies".

1787 French chemist Antoine Lavoisier defined a chemical element as "the last point which analysis can reach". He listed all the known elements and introduced chemical symbols, such as O for oxygen, which we still use today.

1808 English physicist John Dalton suggested that each pure chemical element had its own kind of atom. This was the forerunner of modern ideas about matter and atoms.

1868–9 Russian scientist Dmitri Mendeleév listed all the known elements, and devised a chart called the Periodic Table (see above) to categorise them all by their similar weights and properties.

H Hydrogen 1																	He Helium 2
Li Lithium 3	Be Beryllium 4											B Boron 5	C Carbon 6	N Nitrogen 7	O Oxygen 8	F Flourine 9	Ne Neon 10
Na Sodium 11	Mg Magnesium 12											Al Aluminium 13	Si Silicon 14	P Phosphorus 15	S Sulphur 16	Cl Chlorine 17	Ar Argon 18
K Potassium 19	Ca Calcium 20	Sc Scandium 21	Ti Titanium 22	V Vanadium 23	Cr Chromium 24	Mn Manganese 25	Fe Iron 26	Co Cobalt 27	Ni Nickel 28	Cu Copper 29	Zn Zinc 30	Ga Gallium 31	Ge Germanium 32	As Arsenic 33	Se Selentium 34	Br Bromine 35	Kr Krypton 36
Rb Rubidium 37	Sr Strontium 38	Y Yttrium 39	Zr Zirconium 40	Nb Niobium 41	Mo Molybdenum 42	Tc Technetium 43	Ru Ruthenium 44	Rh Rhodium 45	Pd Palladium 46	Ag Silver 47	Cd Cadmium 48	In Indium 49	Sn Tin 50	Sb Antimony 51	Te Tellurium 52	I Iodine 53	Xe Xenon 54
Cs Caesium 55	Ba Barium 56		Hf Hafnium 72	Ta Tantalum 73	W Tungsten 74	Re Rhenium 75	Os Osmium 76	Ir Iridium 77	Pt Platanium 78	Au Gold 79	Hg Mercury 80	Tl Thalium 81	Pb Lead 82	Bi Bismuth 83	Po Polonium 84	At Astatine 85	Rn Radon 86
Fr Francium 87	Ra Radium 88		Rf Rutherfordium 104	Db Dubnium 105	Sg Seaborgium 106	Bh Bohrium 107	Hs Hassium 108	Mt Meitnerium 109	Ds Darmstadtium 110	Uuu Unununium 111	Uub Ununbium 112						

	La Lanthanum 57	Ce Cerium 58	Pr Praseodymium 59	Nd Neodymium 60	Pm Promethium 61	Sm Samarium 62	Eu Europium 63	Gd Gadoloinium 64	Tb Terbium 65	Dy Dysprosium 66	Ho Holmium 67	Er Erbium 68	Tm Thulium 69	Yb Ytterbium 70	Lu Lutetium 71
	Ac Actinium 89	Th Thorium 90	Pa Protactinium 91	U Uranium 92	Np Neptunium 93	Pu Plutonium 94	Am Americium 95	Cm Curium 96	Bk Berkelium 97	Cf Californium 98	Es Einsteinium 99	Fm Fermium 100	Md Mendelevium 101	No Nobelium 102	Lr Lawrencium 103

⊕ All the known pure substances are arranged in a chart called the Periodic Table of chemical elements. They are arranged by their properties and weights. The lightest elements are upper left, the heaviest ones are lower right. The different colours represent the different type of element. For example, all the elements known as noble gases are shown in turquoise (first column on right). Each of the elements in this column are extremely stable, which means that they do not react dangerously with other elements.

Each left-to-right row is a period of elements with similar weights

Each top-to-bottom column groups elements with similar properties

What holds the parts of an atom together?

Protons and neutrons are held together in the nucleus by a basic attraction called the strong nuclear force. Protons have a type of electrical force called electric charge, which is positive. Electrons have a negative charge and neutrons have no charge. The positive protons attract the negative electrons and hold them near the nucleus. Most atoms have the same number of protons and electrons, so their charges balance each other. The atom has no charge – it is neutral.

Chlorine atom

Carbon atom

Sodium atom

L shell holds up to 8 electrons

K shell (innermost) holds up to 2 electrons

M shell holds up to 8 electrons

⊕ Scientists once thought that electrons orbited the nucleus at a different distance, like planets orbiting the Sun. Then the idea of 'shells' arose, where groups of electrons stay at a set distance from the nucleus. The modern view is that electrons move from one shell to another.

Are all atoms the same?

Each kind of pure substance, known as a chemical element, has its own kind of atoms, which differ from the atoms of all other elements. So in an element, such as carbon, all the atoms are the same, with the same number of subatomic particles. Oxygen atoms are also all the same, but they differ from carbon atoms, with a different number of subatomic particles. There are more than 100 chemical elements, as shown in the table above. About 30 of these are manufactured.

⊕ Lavoisier began the system of using symbols for chemicals in 1787.

Amazing **atom facts**

- A nanometre is an incredibly small unit – one billionth of a metre. So 10 million atoms in a row would stretch just 2 mm.

- A typical atom is about 0.2 to 0.3 nanometres across.

- The nucleus at the centre of an atom is tiny compared to the size of the whole atom.

- If the whole atom was a massive sports stadium, with the outermost electrons whizzing around the farthest seats, the nucleus would be the size of a human thumb in the middle.

- In a solid substance, the atoms are about 0.3 nanometres apart, so their outermost electrons almost touch.

⊕ Dalton studied gases as well as chemistry, and from the age of 15, he kept daily records of the weather.

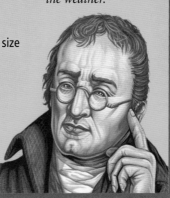

All matter in the Universe is made of the atoms of pure substances, called chemical elements. These atoms join together or can be linked in countless ways to form the common objects and materials that we see and use every day – metals, wood, plastic, glass, water, rocks, soil and even the air around us.

⊙ *Molecules of sodium chloride form crystals of salt, such as table salt, sea salt or rock salt.*

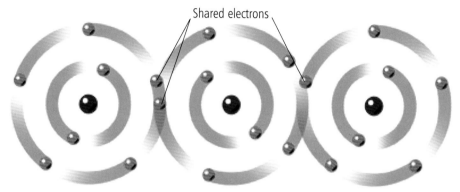

Shared electrons

⬆ *When atoms join by covalent bonds, electrons orbit in one atom for part of the time, and the other for the rest of the time. The three atoms of a water molecule, two hydrogen and one oxygen, H_2O, have covalent bonds, as shown above.*

Do atoms join together?

Atoms usually join or bond with other atoms to form groups called molecules. In some cases the atoms come very close together and 'share' electrons, so that the electron sometimes goes around one nucleus and sometimes around the other. This is a covalent bond. Oxygen atoms floating in the air are joined in pairs by covalent bonds to form oxygen molecules O_2.

Are atoms ever alone?

On Earth, atoms are rarely found alone. Among the few examples are the 'inert gases' – helium, neon, argon, krypton and xenon. 'Inert' means 'inactive'. These gases form a tiny proportion of the air. Their atoms have all the electrons they need, with no need to share or swap. So they hardly ever join or bond, even with each other.

Sodium atom

➜ *In an ionic bond, one or more electrons pass from one atom to another. Molecules of common salt, sodium chloride, form in this way.*

How else do atoms join?

One or more electrons may 'jump' from one atom to a nearby one. This is known as an ionic bond. Atoms of the elements sodium and chlorine are linked by ionic bonds to form molecules of sodium chloride, NaCl, which we know as salt (table or cooking salt). Electrons are negative, so the sodium atom that loses its electron becomes a positive ion. The chlorine atom which receives an electron becomes a negative ion. Positive and negative attract and the sodium and chlorine stay close together.

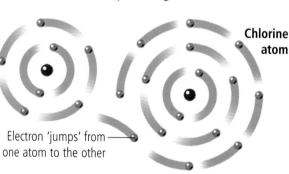

Chlorine atom

Electron 'jumps' from one atom to the other

Nuclear **facts**

Key **dates**

1800s Chemists had studied matter as much as possible. Physicists carried on the search, using methods such as electrical pulses.

1897 English scientist J. J. Thomson discovered particles smaller than atoms, which he called corpuscles. Streams of the particles were known as cathode rays. Today we call them electrons.

1911 New Zealand-born physicist Ernest Rutherford suggested that each atom had a tiny, heavy nucleus at its centre, with electrons circling it.

1912–13 Danish scientist Niels Bohr devised the 'shell' idea of an atom, that electrons move at certain distances from the nucleus of the atom, within separate 'shells'.

1919 Rutherford succeeded in breaking apart the nucleus, a process called 'splitting the atom'.

1932 English physicist James Chadwick discovered the neutron particle inside the nucleus of an atom.

1942 A team led by Enrico Fermi carried out the first 'chain reaction' of atomic fission – where nuclei split apart, releasing huge amounts of energy, causing more nuclei to split.

1945 The science of splitting atoms was used to make two atomic bombs, which were dropped on the Japanese cities of Hiroshima and Nagasaki, ending the Second World War.

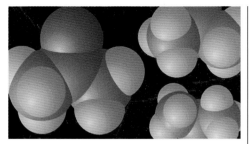

⬆ *The substance called acetone, also known as propanone, is commonly used in nail varnish remover. Each molecule of acetone has three carbon atoms (orange), one oxygen (pink) and six hydrogen (light green). It is written as the formula CH_3COCH_3.*

What is a compound?

A compound is a molecule with atoms from different chemical elements, rather than from the same chemical element. For example, an oxygen molecule, O_2, is not a compound. However, a salt molecule, NaCl, is a compound, because it consists of two or more different chemical elements. Most everyday substances are made from compounds.

⬆ *The tall towers at an oil refinery split crude oil into all its 'fractions'.*

How many atoms are in a compound?

The number varies from a few, to millions. Some substances, such as salt, have molecules with just two atoms each. If each sodium chloride molecule in a tiny grain of salt was increased to the size of the dot on this 'i', then the salt grain would be more than 2 km high. Other substances, such as plastic and wood, have giant molecules consisting of millions of atoms. Many of these are based on the element carbon. Carbon can join with up to four other atoms, so that it forms thousands of different compounds. Especially common are combinations of carbon and hydrogen, called hydrocarbons (CHs), and those of carbon, hydrogen and oxygen known as carbohydrates (CHOs).

➡ *Crude oil or petroleum, straight from the ground, is a mixture of hundreds of compounds. In an oil refinery it is heated so that it splits up into the gases of these compounds. These gases are turned back into liquids at various temperatures, at different levels in a tall tower called a fractionation column.*

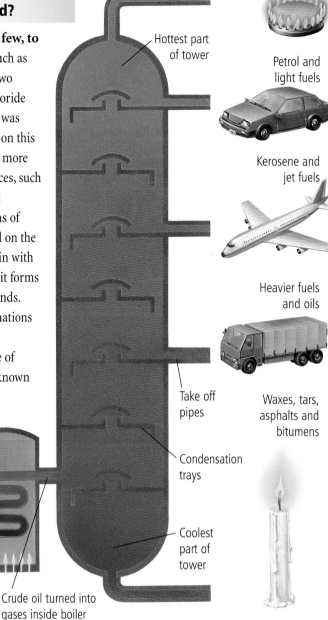

Fuel gases

Petrol and light fuels

Kerosene and jet fuels

Heavier fuels and oils

Waxes, tars, asphalts and bitumens

Hottest part of tower

Take off pipes

Condensation trays

Coolest part of tower

Crude oil turned into gases inside boiler

⬆ *Rutherford worked on radioactive rays and energy as well as atoms and nuclear fusion.*

⬅ *A nuclear explosion's vast energy comes from energy within atoms.*

Bigger and bigger

Natural gas and petroleum oil contain many compounds of the type known as hydrocarbons. They form larger and larger molecules. The simplest is methane, with one carbon and four hydrogen atoms, written as CH_4. It is also given off by decay and known as 'marsh gas'. Next simplest is ethane, with two carbon and six hydrogen atoms (CH_3CH_3). Ethane is found in natural gas and used for refrigeration. Propane has three carbon and eight hydrogen atoms ($CH_3CH_2CH_3$). It is a common fuel in tanks and 'bottle' cylinders. Also relatively simple is butane, with four carbon and ten hydrogen atoms ($CH_3CH_2CH_2CH_3$). It is also a valuable fuel gas. There are many more compounds.

⬇ *In about 1912, Niels Bohr devised the beginnings of what scientists now call quantum theory.*

Science plays a huge part in the items we use every day – cars, televisions, tools, appliances, buildings, even furniture and clothing. They are all made from specially chosen materials, ranging from natural wood or stone to high-tech composites. Materials scientists specialize in putting together atoms, molecules and substances to create the right material for each job.

⬆ *Copper is especially efficient at carrying or conducting electricity, it is second only to silver. It is braided so that it can be bent many times without cracking.*

How is a material's strength measured?

It depends, because there are different kinds of 'strength'. Tensile strength resists pulling or stretching, compression strength resists pressing or squeezing, and torsional strength resists twisting. These different kinds of strength are measured by putting pieces of a material into a very powerful machine, a hydraulic test rig, which pulls, squashes or turns them until they crack and break. Every substance or material has a different combination of these strengths, suitable for different purposes.

What are other features of materials?

Another feature is flexibility or bendiness, which is the opposite of stiffness or rigidity. This is linked to elasticity – whether a material springs back to its original shape after being bent. Weight is another feature, especially density, which is the amount of weight in a certain volume. Durability is how long a material can last. A material is also categorized by its ability to conduct electricity.

What are natural materials?

Natural materials are found around us, as part of nature, rather than being artificial or manufactured. Wood is a natural material and is important in making furniture, utensils and structures such as houses and bridges. Various kinds of rock and stone are also widely used, especially in the construction of larger buildings. Natural fibres, such as cotton, are woven into fabrics for clothes, curtains and other items.

⬆ *Wood is often used in the construction of houses or boats, because it is a strong and durable material that can last against elements, such as strong winds and rain.*

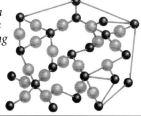

⬅ *Materials that carry heat or electricity, such as a metal spoon in a cup of hot liquid, are thermal or electrical conductors. Those that do not are insulators, such as a ceramic mug.*

More about materials

Glass as a material
Glass is among the most useful of all materials. Various types of glass are made by heating the natural substances of sand (silica), limestone and soda-ash, with other ingredients. Glass is sometimes used as a structural material, to take strain, but it is very brittle, and under too much strain it can crack or shatter. It is widely-used as an insulator for heat and electricity – and for windows because it is see-through or transparent.

Plastics as polymers
Many plastics are polymers. A polymer molecule is a large molecule made by joining or stringing together many identical smaller molecules, known as monomers, like the links in a chain.

➡ *Glass is known as an amorphous material, meaning its atoms do not have a regular arrangement or pattern.*

Polymers

Polyethylene – often known by the trade name Polythene. It is slightly 'waxy' to touch. It is used for packaging, toys, pipes, tubes and wire covering.

Polystyrene – It is 'expanded' or 'blown' to contain bubbles of air and used for lightweight packaging and heat insulation, or in solid form for kitchen utensils.

Polyurethane – This is also blown or foamed with air bubbles and used for lining materials and padding in furniture.

What material is most commonly used?

One commonly-used material is steel, an alloy (combination) of various substances based on the metal, iron. Pure metals are also widely used, such as very light aluminium, for items ranging from aircraft to drink cans. Copper is used as a conductor of electricity in wires. Most materials in modern products are made by various industrial processes rather than being obtained from nature.

Iron ore, coke and limestone

➡ *Specialist metals are heated in furnaces and carefully hand-poured into moulds, where they cool and solidify into the required shape. Brass is an alloy (mixture) of copper and zinc.*

➡ *Iron is obtained by heating iron ore in a blast furnace, and pouring off the wastes or slag. Pure iron is often combined with carbon and other substances to make steel.*

Hot gases to super-heater

Super-heated iron ore and limestone (the coke burns to create the heat)

Super-heated air blows into furnace

Slag

Molten iron ore

Is a tin can really made of tin?

Only the outer coating is made of tin. A 'tin' can is mainly steel, but steel can rust. So the steel can is coated with a thin layer of the metal, tin, which does not rust and so protects the steel beneath it.

⬅ *Many metals and minerals form crystals as they cool from liquid to solid. The cooling process must be carefully controlled so the crystals lock together well for strength. Random-sized crystals would cause weakness in the material. Most crystals are tiny, only visible under a magnifying glass or microscope.*

➡ *Bullet-proof vests are woven from an immensely strong fibre, called kevlar, to withstand the impact of bullets.*

⬇ *Fast vehicles, such as racing cars, speedboats and jet planes contain many composites, each manufactured to have the right mix of strength, weight, stiffness and other features.*

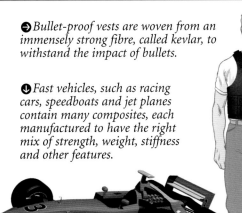

Amazing **facts**

- Composites are combinations of single materials, which combine the best features of each material, in order to create materials specialized for certain jobs.

- One common example of a composite is GRP, glass-reinforced plastic, commonly called 'glass-fibre'.

- GRP has strands or fibres of glass, for rigidity and toughness, surrounded by a resin of plastic for some flexibility and resistance to shattering and corrosion.

- Many composites contain the material called carbon fibre, which is very thin, silky-black strands of pure carbon.

- Carbon fibre has four times more tensile strength than steel and is mixed with plastic resins to make some of the strongest and lightest of all composite materials.

Our world is driven by energy. Without energy the world would be dark, cold, still and silent. We use it in many forms, including movement, sound, chemical bonds, electricity, heat, light, waves and rays. Energy is needed for anything to happen and it can be converted from its current form to various other forms to be used.

A typical power station changes chemical energy in the fuel into heat, then movement and then electricity. But some of the fuel energy is converted into excess heat, which is spread into the air by huge cooling towers.

Where is energy?

Energy is everywhere and exists in everything. It has many forms. Chemical energy is released during chemical reactions. Food is a store of chemical energy, and when eaten can be used to power the movements of the human body. Potential energy is stored energy, ready to be used and converted into kinetic (movement) energy. Electrical energy is when a form of energy is converted into electricity. Solar energy comes from the Sun. There are many forms of energy.

Wind turbines convert the kinetic energy of moving air into electricity. The wind obtained its energy in the form of heat from the Sun. In fact, nearly all the energy we use on Earth, in one form or another, comes from the Sun. Wind turbines generate their energy in a sustainable way, without using up valuable fuel resources.

Can energy be made or destroyed?

A basic law of science says that energy cannot be created from nothing and equally cannot disappear. This applies throughout the Universe. However, energy can be changed from one form to another. For example, when a rocket takes off, the chemical energy in its fuel is changed into other forms of energy, such as heat, light, sound and movement energy. Energy can also be spread out so that it becomes weaker. When we say we 'use' energy, we mean that we convert some of it into the type we need. This generally converts the rest into a less useful type of energy that we cannot use. However, scientists say that energy is 'conserved' because the total amount of energy is always the same.

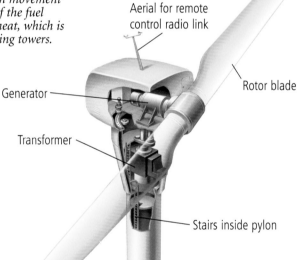

Aerial for remote control radio link

Rotor blade

Generator

Transformer

Stairs inside pylon

Using energy

Changing energy

In science, energy is the ability or capacity to do work or to cause change. Work is usually described as the changing of energy from one form or system to another, often resulting in some type of movement. In everyday life we think of 'work' as something useful, with a purpose. But this is not so in science. For example, an apple hanging on a tree has the type of energy known as potential energy, because of its position high above the ground. If the apple falls, its potential energy is changed into the energy of movement, known as kinetic energy, and 'work' has been done in the process, as it fell from the tree. This work happens whether the apple falls to the ground, or if it hits something on its way down.

Potential energy is found in a bird as it sits on a perch before flying away. The potential energy becomes kinetic energy once the bird takes off into the air.

What happens in an energy chain?

An energy chain is the conversion of different forms of energy into a form that can be used. For example, coal, which is found deep underground, has a store of chemical energy. When burnt, this chemical energy becomes heat energy, which is used to make steam by heating water. The steam turns turbines to produce kinetic energy. This kinetic energy is converted in a machine called a generator in the power station to become electrical energy. Electrical energy is sent to homes and offices where it is used for light, and to power applicances, such as televisions and computers.

A waterwheel changes the kinetic energy of running water into useful mechanical energy, to drive machines such as millstones, which grind grain into flour.

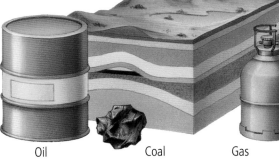
Common fuels we burn for energy include oil, coal and gas. These were formed by the fossilization of decayed plants and other life-forms long ago. Their energy came as light from the Sun. Oil and coal are extracted from deep in the ground, formed beneath rock layers.

Oil   Coal   Gas

Can energy be created from atoms?

Energy can be made in one way – from matter or mass. Atoms, or usually parts of atoms, can be changed into energy. The different parts of atoms, such as neutrons, cease to exist in their current form and instead there is a large amount of energy in their place. The scientific law regarding the conservation of mass and energy states that any process or event has the same amount of mass and energy at the end as there was at the beginning of the process.

What is nuclear energy?

Nuclear energy is created in reactors inside nuclear power stations, nuclear-powered submarines, some spacecraft, and also in nuclear explosions. Nuclear fuel, such as uranium, generates enormous amounts of heat energy from the 'destruction' of the parts of its atoms. The energy produced is called nuclear energy because it comes from splitting the nucleus of an atom.

Nuclear energy comes from the splitting or fission of the nuclei (centres) of atoms in nuclear fuel, such as uranium or plutonium. A fast-moving neutron smashes apart the nucleus, releasing heat, other forms of energy, and also more neutrons, which enable the fission process to continue.

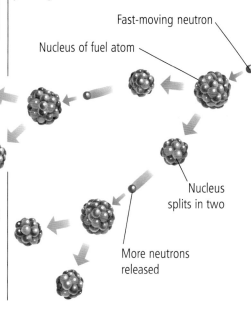

Fast-moving neutron

Nucleus of fuel atom

Nucleus splits in two

More neutrons released

Measuring **energy**

About 100 billion joules of energy is needed to launch a spacecraft.

- The main unit for measuring both energy and work is the joule.

- An older unit was the calorie, which was used especially to measure heat energy and the chemical energy contained in foods.

- One calorie equals 4.2 joules, and one kilocalorie or kcal (also written as 'Calorie' with a capital 'C') equals 4,200 joules (4.2 kJ).

- A 100-watt light bulb requires one joule of electrical energy each second.

- A typical light bulb left on for 24 hours takes about 5 million joules.

- An average person needs about 5 to 10 million joules of energy each day from foods, to stay active and healthy.

- A split-second bolt of lightning releases 2,000 million joules.

- A large earthquake releases about 10 million million million joules in just a few seconds.

When we switch on a light, turn on the computer, listen to the radio or watch television, we rely on our most convenient form of energy – electricity. It is convenient because it can be sent easily along wires and cables. Also it is readily changed into many other forms of energy, including light, heat, sound and movement.

◀ *Electrical energy or charge does not always flow. It can build up on the surface of an insulator, for example, after rubbing a plastic comb. This charge is called 'static electricity' and it attracts very light items, such as bits of tissue paper.*

What is electricity?

Electricity is the movement or flow of the tiny parts of atoms called electrons, which have an electric charge. Electrons move around the central nucleus of an atom. But if an electron receives enough energy it can break away from its atom and 'hop' to the next one, where an electron has also broken away and jumped to the next atom, and so on. These moving electrons represent energy. As billions of them hop in the same direction from atom to atom, they cause a flow of electric current.

◀ *Electric current only flows if it has a pathway or circuit of conductors from its source and back again. Here, the circuit includes two wires and a bulb. The wires move the current to the bulb and back again.*

▶ *Electricity flows along a wire as electrodynamic charge. If it has nowhere to flow, it collects on the surface of an object as electrostatic charge (known as static electricity). Van de Graaff generators (such as the one shown here) build up charges of millions of volts, which finally leap away as giant sparks.*

Do all substances carry electricity?

No, only certain substances carry electricity. These substances are called conductors. Most metals, especially silver and gold, carry electricity well. Many other substances do not carry electricity. Instead, they have a high resistance to its flow and are known as insulators. They include wood, glass, plastic, paper, card and ceramics, such as pottery. Electrical wires usually have a conducting core of metal strands surrounded by a plastic sheath for insulation, which prevents the electricity from leaking.

Electrical units

◀ *A portable multimeter can be adjusted to measure volts, amps, ohms and other electrical units. It is a vital piece of equipment for electricians and electrical engineers. The meter is used to check safety equipment and ensure that electricity is not flowing to parts of machines that people touch, which would make the machines unsafe.*

How long?

For the same amount of electricity, these gadgets and appliances would run for the following lengths of time:

'Instant' hot-water shower	10–15 mins
Electric heater (convector)	1 hr
Hair-dryer on maximum setting	1–1.5 hrs
Washing machine	2 hrs
Large freezer	3 hrs
Standard television	3–5 hrs
Electric blanket	6 hrs
100-watt light bulb	10 hrs
Electric shaver	70 hrs

How do batteries work?

Batteries change chemical energy into electrical energy. The links or bonds between atoms in chemical substances contain energy. As these break down in a chemical reaction, their energy passes to the electrons in the atoms and makes them move. This happens in a battery, but only when the electrons have somewhere to go, such as along a pathway or circuit of wires and components.

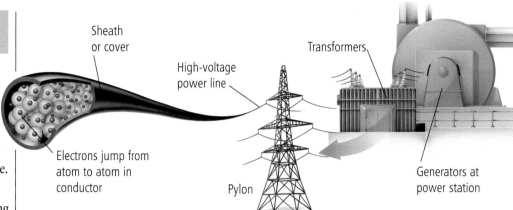

Sheath or cover

High-voltage power line

Transformers

Electrons jump from atom to atom in conductor

Pylon

Generators at power station

⬆ *The flow of electricity is the movement of millions of electrons, which jump between atoms in the conductor – usually copper wire.*

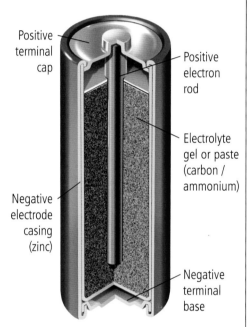

Positive terminal cap

Positive electron rod

Electrolyte gel or paste (carbon / ammonium)

Negative electrode casing (zinc)

Negative terminal base

⬆ *A typical torch battery consists of two contacts or electrodes: the positive anode and negative cathode, with chemicals between them called the electrolyte. Chemical reactions between the electrodes and electrolyte cause the current to flow.*

What happens inside a power station?

In some power stations fuels such as coal, oil or gas are burned to make heat. This boils water into steam, which blasts past the fan-shaped blades or rotors of a turbine and makes them spin. The turbine is linked to a generator, inside which is a magnetic field, which rotates near a coil of wire, and this makes electricity in the wire. In hydro-electric power stations, running water spins the turbine blades. In wind turbines the propeller-like blades are whirled around by the wind to generate electricity.

What are DC and AC?

DC is direct current electricity and AC is alternating current electricity. Direct current electricity flows steadily in the same direction while alternating current electricity rapidly changes direction and flows one way then the other, 50 or 60 times each second. Batteries make DC. The mains electricity from wall sockets and light fittings is AC.

Transformers

⬅ *Electricity from power stations is sent along huge cables, high above the ground, or buried below the surface. Its voltage is reduced by transformers, from hundreds of thousands of volts to only a few thousand for large factories, and just hundreds for homes, offices and schools.*

Measuring **electricity**

Electricity is measured in various ways by special scientific units.

- Amps (amperes, A) are the amount or quantity of electrical flow. One amp is about 6 billion billion electrons flowing past each second.

- Volts (v) is the pushing strength or force of electricity, also called EMF, electromotive force. A typical torch battery is 1.5 volts, a car battery 12 volts, mains electricity in many countries such as France and the USA is 110 volts, and in the UK it is 220–240 volts.

- Ohms (Ω) measure the resistance of flow to electricity. A 1-m length of a good conductor, such as copper wire, has almost no ohms, while the same length of a good insulator, such as wood, has millions.

- Watts measure power, which in science is the rate at which energy is changed or converted. One watt is one joule of energy per second.

- An ordinary light bulb is 60 or 100 watts, and a room heater 1,000 watts.

- Watts can be used to measure any form of energy use, not just electrical energy. For example, a person jogging along requires about 500 watts, while a family car produces about 100,000 watts.

- An older unit for power is horsepower, hp. One unit of horsepower is equivalent to 746 watts.

- When generating electricity, a typical wind turbine produces about one megawatt (millions of watts). The biggest hydro-electric power stations produce more than 10,000 megawatts.

Magnets have no effect on many substances, such as wood, paper, plastic and even some metals, such as the aluminium used in drink cans. Yet when they are near an iron-based object, they pull it towards them with an invisible force. And when two magnets are near each other, they may attract (pull each other together) or repel (push each other apart).

North Pole

South Pole

Magnetism at its strongest at the pole

Lines of magnetic force

A typical bar magnet is made of steel. Its lines of magnetic force curve from one pole to the other at each end. But a magnet can be any shape, including a u-like horseshoe, a disc with a pole on each side, or a ring with one pole on the outer rim and one on the inner.

What is a magnet?

A magnet is an object that produces a force called magnetism. The area where the force is felt is called the magnetic field. The force is strongest at two places in the magnet, called poles. The two poles are not the same, in fact they are opposites. One is called north or + and the other is called south or −. When two magnets come near, the north pole of one pushes or repels the north pole of the other, but pulls or attracts the south pole. The basic law of magnetism is that like poles repel, unlike poles attract.

How is magnetism made?

It is due to the movements of the same particles that cause electricity – the electrons of atoms. Electrons orbit their atom's nucleus, and spin around while the nucleus spins, too. Normally electrons spin in random ways, at different angles. But in a magnet it is believed that the electron spins are lined up, so their tiny forces combine to create the force of magnetism.

Which substances are magnetic?

A magnetic substance is one that is attracted by a magnet. The most common magnetic substance is iron. Steel contains mainly iron, so steel is magnetic too. A few less common metals are slightly magnetic, such as nickel and cobalt, and the much rarer metals, such as neodymium, gadolinium and dysprosium.

The type of iron-rich rock called magnetite or lodestone has natural magnetism. Long, slim pieces of it were used for the first direction-finding magnetic compasses.

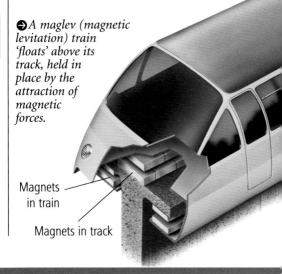

A maglev (magnetic levitation) train 'floats' above its track, held in place by the attraction of magnetic forces.

Magnets in train

Magnets in track

Magnetic **attraction**

The Earth as a magnet
Planet Earth is itself an enormous magnet. It has a core of iron-rich rocks at its centre, at immense pressure and temperature. The core is so hot that it flows like treacle. As the Earth spins around once each day the core flows and swishes, too, and the moving iron generates a magnetic field. This field extends around Earth's surface and out into space. Like all magnetic fields, it becomes weaker with distance. The magnetic poles of the Earth are actually some distance from the geographic poles, the North and South Poles. These geographic Poles mark the line of axis around which the planet spins.

Earth's natural magnetism is generated in its core. But the magnetic field extends hundreds of kilometres out into space. The magnetic north pole is near Bathurst Island in northern Canada, more than 1,000 km from the geographic North Pole. The magnetic south pole is in the ocean near Wilkes Land, Antarctica, more than 2,000 km from the geographic South Pole.

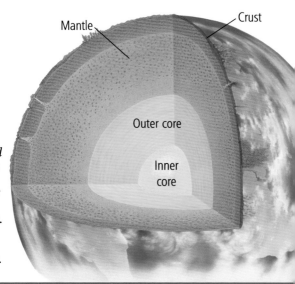

Mantle

Crust

Outer core

Inner core

⬆ *Big electromagnets can lift up heavy loads, such as car engines. They are also used at scrapyards for sorting iron-based or ferrous metals from other metals when recycling.*

Can magnets be switched on and off?

They can if they are electromagnets. Electricity and magnetism are two parts of the same basic or fundamental force, known as electromagnetism. Whenever an electric current flows in a wire, it creates a magnetic field around itself. If a wire is wound into a coil, with a piece of iron in the middle, this makes the magnetic field stronger and is known as an electromagnet. The magnetic field is present when the electricity flows, but when it is switched off, the magnetism disappears in an instant.

Are magnets common?

Very common. They are used in a simple way for holding paper onto appliances such as fridges, as knife-holders, for gathering and holding pins and nails, and as magnetic catches for doors. Large magnets are found in loudspeakers. Electromagnetism is used in many devices, such as remote-control cars, locks, electric generators and motors, videotapes, television sets, computers and their magnetic disc drives. Magnets are used in hundreds of different devices.

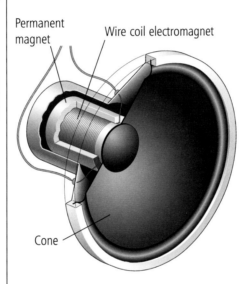

⬆ *A loudspeaker is a device that changes an electric current into sound. Electrical signals flow through a wire coil and turn it into an electromagnet, which pushes and pulls against a permanent magnet to produce sound.*

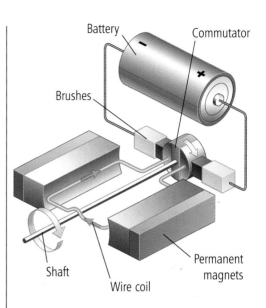

⬆ *A simple DC motor consists of a wire coil on a shaft between two magnetic poles. As it turns, the electric current flowing through the spinning wire coil is reversed by a barrel-shaped commutator switch.*

How does an electric motor work?

Using the push and pull of magnetism. A coil of wire inside an electric motor is positioned near two magnets. As the current flows, the wire becomes an electromagnet and its field interacts with the magnetic field of the surrounding magnets. The pushing and pulling forces produced by the magnets move the wire and so the motor spins. A rotating switch, the commutator, makes the flow of current through the coil change each turn to keep the motor spinning.

Magnets save lives!

The device called a compass is a long, slim magnet that can turn or swivel freely. It follows the basic law of magnetism so that each of its poles attracts the Earth's opposite magnetic pole. This makes the compass line up with the Earth's magnetic field and point north-south. Countless lives have been saved as explorers, sailors, pilots, mountaineers and numerous travellers have used the magnetic compass to find their way to safety. Today, travellers may use satellite navigation receivers, but they may break or run out of electricity so the magnetic compass is still carried as a standby.

⬆ *The dial of a magnetic compass is turned around so that its north lines up with the compass needle. A map held next to the compass is then also moved around so that it lines up too. Maps are usually produced with north at the top.*

Flipping poles

As certain types of rocks melt and then cool and solidify in the Earth's crust (outer layer), tiny amounts of magnetism are 'frozen' into them. This magnetism is lined up with the Earth's natural magnetic field. Different layers of rock, formed over millions of years, show how the Earth's magnetic poles have moved about, and even 'flipped' or reversed, so that north became south, and south turned into north. This has happened many times throughout Earth's history. This type of information helps to determine the age of rocks and the fossils of dinosaurs and other prehistoric animals found within the rocks.

Electronic gadgets are all around us, from televisions, computers and mobile phones to washing machines and cars. Electronics is one of the fastest-growing areas of science, as the electronic chip becomes smaller and smaller, yet faster and more powerful.

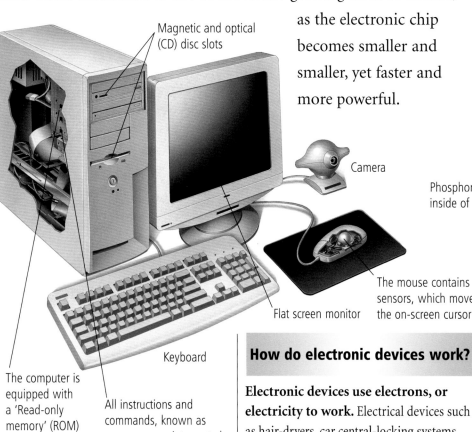

Magnetic and optical (CD) disc slots

Camera

The mouse contains sensors, which move the on-screen cursor

Flat screen monitor

Keyboard

The computer is equipped with a 'Read-only memory' (ROM)

All instructions and commands, known as programs, are interpreted and carried out in the CPU

Electron guns

Aerial

Focusing and scanning coils

Phosphor dots on inside of screen

Glass vacuum tube

⊕ *One of the smallest components in a typical personal computer is the central processing unit (CPU), where microprocessors interpret commands. The items connected by wires, called peripherals, include the keyboard, mouse, screen (monitor) and additional devices, such as scanners or cameras.*

⊕ *In a standard TV set, 'guns' fire streams of electrons at the inside of the screen. The electrons hit tiny dots of phosphor chemicals whose glow can be seen from the other side of the screen as the image. There is one electron gun for each set of coloured dots – red, green and blue. The beams pass electromagnetic coils or plates, which make the beams bend or deflect to scan the screen line by line.*

How do electronic devices work?

Electronic devices use electrons, or electricity to work. Electrical devices such as hair-dryers, car central-locking systems, food processors and microwave ovens often have moving parts, such as motors, electromagnets and gears, that we can usually see. They are electromechanical and so are powered by electricity. Electronic devices, such as transistors, have no moving parts except electrons, which are too small to see.

Do electronic devices use much electricity?

The electrons in an electronic device flow as an electric current, which is usually tiny. They measure from a few volts in strength down to only thousandths of a volt, and only fractions of an amp (measure of electrical amount). The electrons are mainly controlled by other electrons, as tiny electrical pulses or by magnetic effects.

Electronic **advances**

⊕ *Apple iMac computers were purpose-designed for electronic information transfer (e-mail and the Internet).*

Key **dates**

1904	Ambrose Fleming made one of the earliest electronic devices, the diode valve.
1906	Lee de Forest developed the triode valve, which worked as an amplifier.
1923	Vladimir Zworykin developed early versions of the electron-scanning television camera and screen.
1946–7	A team, led by William Shockley, invented the transistor, which could amplify electrical signals.
1958	Jack Kilby made several transistors on one piece of semiconductor – an early intergrated circuit.
1962	The first 'microchips' or integrated circuits were mass produced.
1971	The first central processing unit microchips were developed.
1981	Early versions of the IBM PC (personal computer) were introduced.
1988	Mobile phones were introduced.
1996	Playstation computer games.
1998	Apple iMac computers.

What are ICs?

An IC – integrated circuit – is a circuit board where all the components and connections are made at the same time, fully joined together or integrated. Microscopic in size, the circuit can be made up of thousands of individual components. The components, such as switches, resistors, capacitors and transistors, are connected by wires or metal strips on the circuit board.

⬇ *A PCB, printed circuit board, is made with all the metal connectors in position or 'printed' onto the insulator board. Microchips and other components are connected by inserting their metal 'legs' into sockets.*

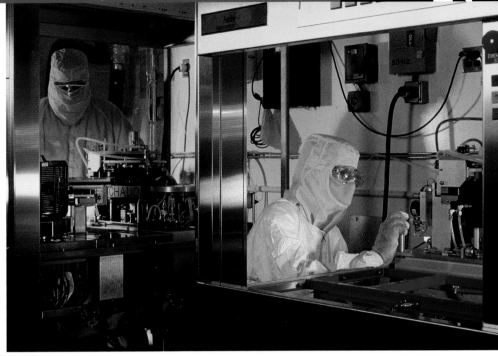

⬆ *Electronic components must be made in extremely clean conditions. A few specks of dust could get inside the components and ruin the manufacture of microchips and electrical circuit boards.*

What is a microchip?

The 'chip' is a slice of a semiconductor material such as silicon and 'micro' means that all the components and connections of the integrated circuit on the chip are microscopic in size. Tiny parts of this material either carry electricity or not, depending on conditions such as changing temperature, or the presence or absence of electricity or magnetism nearby.

Integrated circuit

Plastic casing for insulation

'Leg' connecting pins

What are CPUs?

Central processing unit microchips are the 'brains' of electronic devices, such as computers. Information is fed into the CPU as patterns of millions of tiny electrical signals per second. The microcircuits in the CPU analyze or process the signals and 'decide' what to do according to a set of rules built into the circuit design. The results are fed out as more electrical signals to various other parts of the equipment.

Electronic **components**

Resistor – resists the flow of electricity, and reduces its voltage.

Capacitor – stores electrical energy and charge.

Diode – allows electrical flow one way only.

Potentiometer – resistor adjusted to control, measure or compare voltages.

Transformer – changes voltage (up or down) and alters current to flow in the opposite way.

Photovoltaic cell – turns light energy directly into electricity.

Transistor – adaptable component which can be an amplifier, switch or an oscillator, which makes current flow one way then the other very rapidly.

➜ *Computer-aided special effects can be extended into entire animated adventures.*

Amazing **electronic facts**

• In the early 1970s, the CPUs or microprocessor chips inside the first home computers contained about 8,000 transistors each.

• By the early 2000s, over 40 million transistors can be found in the same-sized chip, and work a thousand times faster than the first ones.

• In general, computing ability doubles in speed and power every 18 months. This is called Moore's law, named after Gordon Moore who suggested it would happen in 1965.

The air around us is full of rays and waves. We can only see one kind of them – light. The others include radio waves, microwaves, heat rays and even tiny amounts of X-rays. These are invisible, yet they are very similar to light rays in every feature, except for the length of each actual wave.

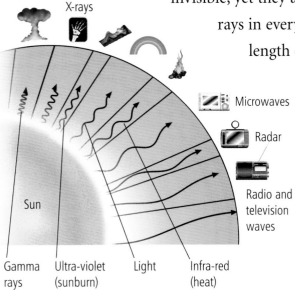

X-rays

Microwaves

Radar

Radio and television waves

Sun

Gamma rays

Ultra-violet (sunburn)

Light

Infra-red (heat)

Nearly all forms of electromagnetic radiation are given off by the Sun. As the wavelengths become smaller, from radio to gamma rays, the frequency – the number of waves per second – becomes larger. We also use many of these waves in various kinds of equipment, such as radio transmitters and microwave ovens.

Can radiation be emitted as particles, not waves?

Some types of radiation are emitted as particles. One type is known as alpha radiation, which is a stream of particles from inside atoms. Each alpha particle consists of two protons and two neutrons (similar to the nucleus of an atom of the very light gas, helium, which also contains two protons and two neutrons). Another type is beta particles, where each particle is an electron (or its 'opposite', a positron).

What is radiation?

Radiation is energy that is given out, or radiated, from a source. One type of radiation is a combination of electricity and magnetism, as electromagnetic waves. These are like up-and-down waves of energy. The different lengths of waves have different names, but they are all the same form of energy. We use them in hundreds of different ways, in communications, medicine, industry and scientific research.

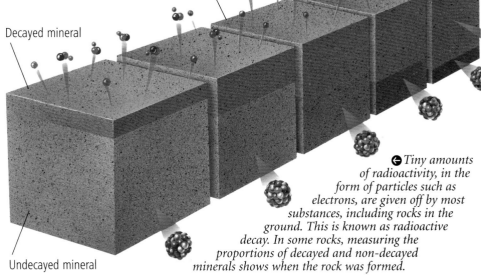

Nuclei of atoms become lighter

Alpha particles

Beta particles

Decayed proportion enlarges

Decayed mineral

Undecayed mineral

Tiny amounts of radioactivity, in the form of particles such as electrons, are given off by most substances, including rocks in the ground. This is known as radioactive decay. In some rocks, measuring the proportions of decayed and non-decayed minerals shows when the rock was formed.

Waves and rays

As the length of electromagnetic waves become shorter, their frequency (number of waves per second) becomes higher. More waves per second can carry more information, for example, as the on-off pulses of digital code in a computer.

X-ray images show up the denser or harder parts of the body, such as bones and teeth, as white or pale against the dark background of softer, fleshy parts.

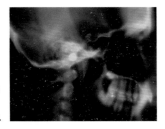

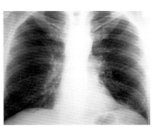

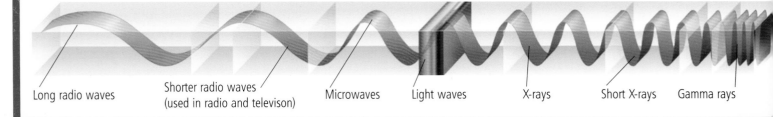

Long radio waves

Shorter radio waves (used in radio and televison)

Microwaves

Light waves

X-rays

Short X-rays

Gamma rays

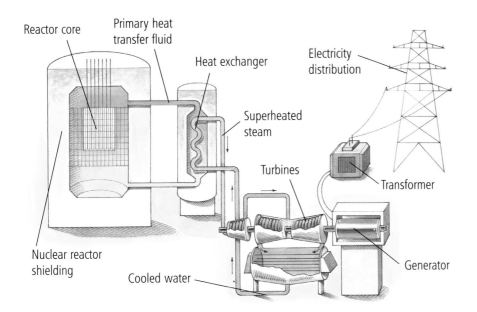

Reactor core
Primary heat transfer fluid
Heat exchanger
Electricity distribution
Superheated steam
Turbines
Transformer
Generator
Nuclear reactor shielding
Cooled water

Is 'radioactivity' radiation?

Yes, radioactivity is energy given off by atoms that are not stable or 'settled', because their subatomic particles are out of balance. Substances that naturally have a proportion of unstable atoms include radium, uranium and plutonium. These substances give off alpha and beta particles and gamma rays, which are extremely short electromagnetic waves.

⊙ *In a nuclear power station, the radiation given out by the splitting of fuel atoms includes vast amounts of heat. This boils water into high-pressure steam that spins turbine blades linked to the generator.*

How fast does radiation travel?

Radiation travels faster than anything else in the Universe. Its electromagnetic waves include light, and nothing can exceed the speed of light in a vacuum (such as the nothingness of space) – which travels about 300,000 km/sec. Many electromagnetic waves travel this fast – equivalent to seven times around the world in less than one second.

⊙ *If an electron beam is fired at certain metal objects, the beam gives off X-rays, which can penetrate solid objects, such as a hand, and cast an image of the interior, such as the bones inside a finger.*

Is radiation harmful?

Generally, no, but some types can be in certain amounts. Ultra-violet rays from the Sun can cause sunburn and skin cancers. Too many X-rays can damage the microscopic cells of living things and lead to illness, tumours and cancers. However, used very carefully, X-rays can also destroy growths and cancers: this is known as radiotherapy. Radioactivity may cause burns, sickness and many other ill effects. Too much of any radiation can be damaging. But in daily life, most forms of radiation are controlled in their amounts and strengths so as not to cause harm to living things.

⊙ *The magnetron in a microwave oven produces the type of radiation known as microwaves. The waves are up to 20 cm in length. They bounce or reflect off the paddles of the stirrer to spread evenly inside the oven.*

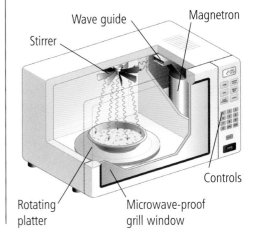

Wave guide
Magnetron
Stirrer
Controls
Rotating platter
Microwave-proof grill window

The EM spectrum

The full range of electromagnetic waves and rays is known as the EM spectrum. The parts differ in the lengths of their waves:

Radio waves – Each wave more than 1 km long to less than 10 m.
Radio waves – (very short, used for television) 10 to less than 1 m.
Microwaves – About 1 m to 1 mm.
Infra-red waves or rays – (carry heat energy) 1 mm to less than 1 micrometre (one-thousandth of 1 ml).
Light waves or rays – (visible light) About 0.8 to 0.4 micrometres.
Ultra-violet rays – 0.1 to 0.001 micrometres.
X-rays – 0.001 to 0.00001 micrometres.
Gamma rays – Less than 0.0001 micrometres (0.1 millionths of a mm).

Amazing radiation facts

Different types of radiation pass through different substances, depending on their power:

• Most kinds travel through air easily.

• Radio waves hardly travel through water.

• Light waves are stopped by most solid objects unless they are transparent, such as glass.

• X-rays can travel through fleshy parts of the body, but not through teeth and bones, and so these show up on a medical X-ray image.

• A thick sheet of metal, such as lead, stops most forms of radiation.

Asimple description of light is that it is something we see with our eyes! Light is actually a form of energy, which is made up of electromagnetic waves. It is essential to our lives, so that we can look around to move about, eat, drink, learn and stay safe. We cannot survive in darkness, nor can most animals and plants.

What is light?

Light is a type of energy. We can imagine it as up-and-down waves of the form of energy known as electromagnetism. This is a combination of electricity and magnetism. So light waves are very similar in form to radio waves, microwaves, infra-red, ultra-violet and X-rays. Light waves are so short that about 2,000 of them would stretch just 1 mm.

◑Light bounces or reflects off very smooth surfaces, in the same pattern and at the same angle as the rays hit the surface. This produces what we call a mirror-image. In this image, left and right are reversed. So in a mirror, we do not see our faces as other people see them.

Is light always in the form of waves?

Not always. Light energy also seems to be in the form of tiny 'packets', which are pieces of light energy known as photons, like the stream of bullets from a machine-gun. For some purposes scientists view light as a continuous form of energy, that moves in up-and-down waves. For other purposes, they view it as units of energy called photons. This is known in science as the 'wave-particle duality' of light.

◑Different wavelengths or colours of light are bent or refracted by slightly different amounts as they pass at an angle into a glass prism. The waves spread out and reveal that ordinary 'white' light is really a mixture of all colours, known as the visible light spectrum.

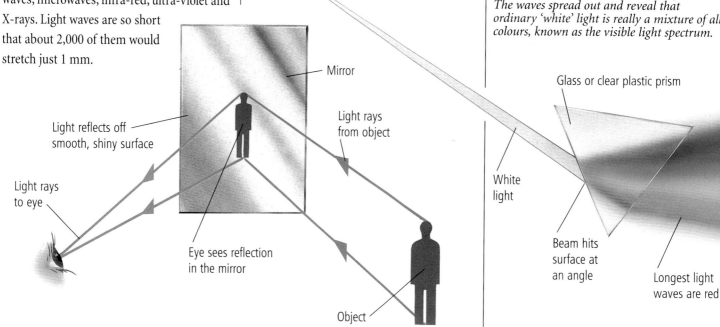

Mirror

Light reflects off smooth, shiny surface

Light rays from object

Light rays to eye

Eye sees reflection in the mirror

Object

Glass or clear plastic prism

White light

Beam hits surface at an angle

Longest light waves are red

Light **fantastic**

Making laser light
'Laser' means 'light amplification by stimulated emission of radiation'. A laser beam is made by putting pulses of energy into a substance called the active medium. The input energy can be electricity, heat or even ordinary light. The atoms of the active medium gain more and more energy, which suddenly reaches a certain limit or threshold, and is given off as a burst of laser light.

➔In one type of laser, energy is put into the active medium of a ruby rod as flashes of ordinary light.

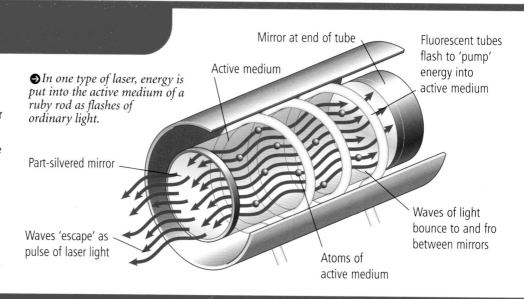

Mirror at end of tube

Active medium

Fluorescent tubes flash to 'pump' energy into active medium

Part-silvered mirror

Waves 'escape' as pulse of laser light

Waves of light bounce to and fro between mirrors

Atoms of active medium

Why are there different colours of light?

The colour of light depends on the length of its waves. The longest ones are each about 770 nanometres (0.00077 mm) in length. Our eyes detect these as red. The shortest light waves are 400 nanometres (0.0004 mm) and our eyes see these as violet. The wavelengths in between form all the other colours, from orange and yellow to green, blue and indigo. This range of colours is known as the light spectrum.

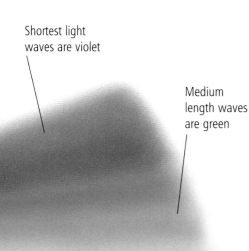

Shortest light waves are violet

Medium length waves are green

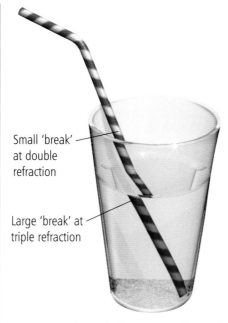

Small 'break' at double refraction

Large 'break' at triple refraction

⬆ *Light rays from the lower straw (beneath the surface of the water) are refracted as they pass through water, glass and air. From the upper straw they pass through only air and glass, so the path of light is different and makes the straw appear broken.*

Does light always travel in straight lines?

If nothing gets in its way, yes. But if light hits any objects or substances, various things can happen. If the object is see-through or transparent, such as a glass window or water, then the light carries on. It may bend where it goes from one transparent substance to another, known as refraction. If an object is opaque (not clear), such as a wooden door, then the light bounces or reflects off it.

How fast is light?

Light has the fastest known speed in the Universe – almost 300,000 km/sec. All electromagnetic waves go at this speed. But this is their speed in a completely empty space or vacuum. The speed of light is affected as it travels through different materials or substances. It travels slower through transparent substances, such as water and glass.

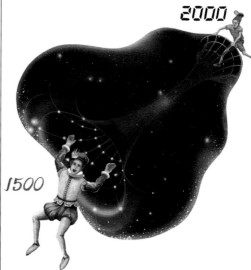

⬆ *One theory about space and time says that as an object moves faster and approaches the speed of light, then the passage of time for that object slows down. At light speed, time stops. Perhaps if the object went faster than light, time would go backwards. 'Short-cuts' in space called wormholes might make faster-than-light speed possible. So travelling through a wormhole could take you back in time, maybe 500 years or more!*

Amazing **facts**

The light of a laser is the same type of electromagnetic wave energy as ordinary light. But it differs in three ways:

Laser light

1 All the light waves are the same length. This means they are the same colour. A laser gives out light of one pure colour only.

2 All of the peaks and troughs of the waves are level or aligned, like the equal 'waves' of corrugated sheet metal.

3 The waves are all parallel, which means they stay the same distance from each other, no matter how far they travel.

Ordinary light

1 Even what seems to be a single colour of light has a mixture of wavelengths, and therefore a mixture of colours.

2 The peaks and troughs are mixed up and not aligned.

3 Waves of ordinary light spread out or diverge so the whole beam gets wider.

Slower **light**

Light speed varies greatly with the substance or medium through which it passes.

Medium	Speed (km/sec)
Vacuum	299,792
Air	299,700
Water	225,000
Window glass	195,000
Decorative (lead crystal) glass	160,000
Diamond	125,000

Loud shouts, soft whispers, repetitive noise, beautiful music, warning sirens, different voices, the crash of thunder – sounds are a huge part of our daily lives. The science of sound is known as acoustics, and it affects the design of modern buildings, as well as a vast variety of products, from televisions and water plumbing to cars, trains and planes.

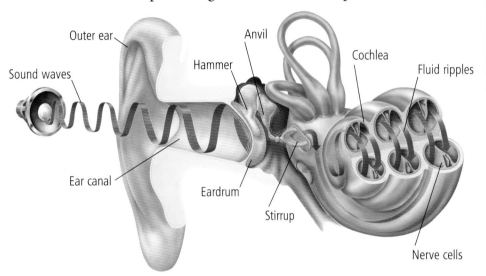

Outer ear

Anvil

Hammer

Cochlea

Sound waves

Fluid ripples

Ear canal

Eardrum

Stirrup

Nerve cells

What is sound?

Sound is energy in the form of movements of a substance or object. The to-and-fro movements many times each second are known as vibrations. Vibrating objects such as a loudspeaker make ripples of waves of high and low air pressure, which travel through the air to our ears. Since sound involves motion, it is a type of kinetic energy.

⬆ Invisible sound waves travel through the air and vibrate the eardrum, which passes the vibrations along the tiny ear bones into the cochlea. The vibrations cause ripples in the fluid within the cochlea, which make nerve signals that are sent to the brain to be processed.

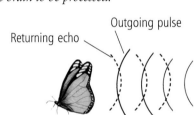

Returning echo

Outgoing pulse

Can we see sounds?

We cannot see sound waves in the air, but we can see big vibrations in solid objects that produce sounds, such as loudspeakers or engines. We can also see the ripples on a liquid such as water, through which sound passes. However, the sounds we hear come from vibrations at the rate of more than 20 per second, known as 20 Hz. Our eyes cannot follow such fast movements so we see just a blur. A butterfly's wingflaps, at 10 Hz (ten per second), are too slow to produce sound for us to hear. A hummingbird's wingbeats at 100 Hz are fast enough to make a buzzing hum, but can only be seen as a blur.

⬇ A bat's squeaks and clicks are mostly ultrasonic – too high for our ears to detect. The sounds reflect from objects around and the bat works out whether the echoes indicate leaves and twigs to be avoided when flying or prey to be caught. This system is called echolocation and allows the bat to fly and feed – even in total darkness.

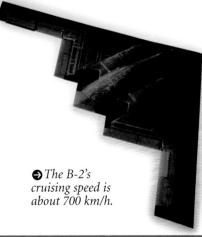

Acoustic **information**

Mach speed
Very fast planes can exceed the speed of sound, known as Mach 1. This causes pressure waves to build up around the craft, which travel away as the loud, deep, dull thud known as sonic boom. The boom would give away the presence of 'stealth' planes, such as this B-2 bomber, which usually flies at just below Mach 1.

➔ The B-2's cruising speed is about 700 km/h.

Amazing **Mach facts**

The speed of sound is measured on the Mach scale. This does not give a speed in m/sec or similar. It gives a comparison number to the speed of sound in certain conditions. The Mach scale is named after German scientist Ernst Mach (1838–1916).

• The speed of sound through air at 20°C and standard air pressure at sea level is about 1,238 km/h. So an object moving this fast would be travelling at Mach 1, while one moving at 1,857 km/h is going at Mach 1.5.

• Very high in the air, where temperature and pressure are lower, the speed of sound is nearer 1,062 km/h. So Mach 1.5 up there is 1,593 km/h.

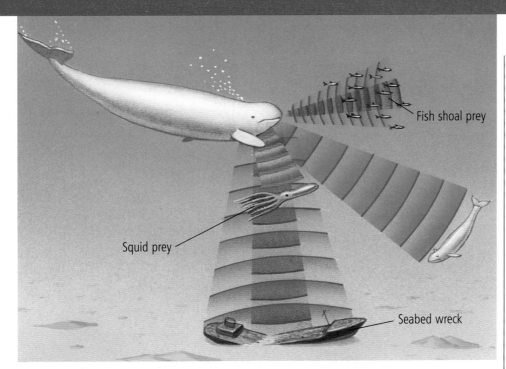

Fish shoal prey

Squid prey

Seabed wreck

Can we hear all sounds?

No, our ears only respond to sounds with vibration speeds between about 20 and 20,000 Hz. The vibration speed or frequency, in Hz, affects the pitch of a sound. Low frequency sounds, such as the roar of a truck or rocket, are very deep and booming. High frequency ones, such as birds singing, are shrill. Sounds lower than about 20 Hz or higher than 20,000 Hz may be all around us, but we cannot hear them.

➲ *Some birdsong can exceed 100,000 Hz.*

➲ *Hunting whales such as the beluga send out sonic clicks. These pulses bounce back as echoes to give the whale information about any objects that might be nearby.*

How fast does sound travel?

The speed of sound depends on what it has to travel through. Its speed in the air varies with air temperature, pressure and humidity (moisture content), travelling an average of 344 m/sec. Sounds move at about 1,500 m/sec through liquids, such as water. It travels even faster through solid objects: 2,500 m/sec through hard plastic, 5,000 m/sec through steel, and about 6,000 m/sec through some types of glass.

Can sound reflect, like light?

Yes, sound waves reflect or bounce off hard, smooth, flat surfaces, such as walls and doors, just as light waves bounce off a mirror. If the returning sound or reflection is more than about one-tenth of a second after the original sound, we hear it separately and call it an echo. If the time gap for the reflection is less, it mixes with the original sound and makes it seem longer, which is known as reverberation.

➲ *It is possible to hear more than one echo from a single sound. This usually occurs in caves, valleys or canyons where there are many different surfaces that can reflect sound. The sound waves bounce from wall to wall and enable us to hear several echoes.*

The decibel **scale**

The energy content of sound is measured in decibels, dB. Sound above 90 dB, especially if high-pitched and long-lasting, can damage hearing.

➲ *In the decibel scale, each gap of 10 dB means a ten-fold increase in energy. For example. 60 dB represents ten times more sound than 50 dB.*

Nuclear explosion
more than 200 dB

Jet plane taking off
120–130 dB

Express train
80–90 dB

People talking
40–60 dB

0   50   100   150   200

10 dB	Quietest sounds our ears detect, such as a ticking watch
20 dB	Average whisper
40 dB	Quiet talking with people nearby
50 dB	Television or radio at average listening volume
60 dB	Fairly loud conversation
70 dB	Appliance such as vacuum cleaner or food processor
80 dB	Train passing through station
100 dB	Very loud machine or tool-like road drill
120 dB	Jet plane at take-off

Machines are all around us, and are often used in everyday life. Jet planes roar overhead, cars whizz past on the road, cranes lift loads, gears are changed on cycles, vacuum cleaners suck and swings and seesaws are used in playgrounds. Machines work because forces make movements.

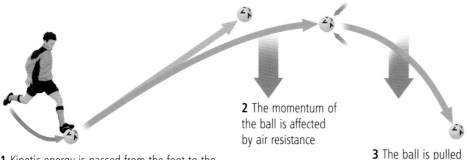

2 The momentum of the ball is affected by air resistance

3 The ball is pulled back down by gravity

1 Kinetic energy is passed from the foot to the ball, applying a force to make the ball move

➊ *The tendency of a moving object to carry on moving in a straight line is counteracted by other forces. For example, air resistance and gravity may act upon a moving object to break its momentum.*

What is a force?

It is a push, pull or other action that makes an object move, or tries to make it move. If you kick a ball, the force from your foot makes the ball move. The kinetic (movement) energy of your foot is passed, or transferred, to the ball. If you kick a wall, the kinetic energy of your foot does not make the wall move, but it is changed into energy that squashes against your foot.

➊ *The basic forms of matter (solid, liquid, gas and plasma) depend on the motion of atoms. Most pure substances can change their form as their temperature changes. For example, water (liquid) becomes ice (solid) when cooled enough, or steam (gas) when heated enough.*

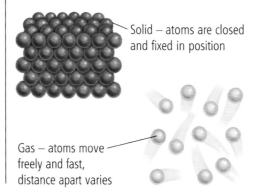

Solid – atoms are closed and fixed in position

Gas – atoms move freely and fast, distance apart varies

Do atoms move?

It depends on the substance or object they are in. If it is a solid, such as iron, or wood, the atoms are almost still and just move or vibrate slightly around a central point. In a liquid, such as water or oil, the atoms can move about, but they stay the same distance from each other, so the liquid keeps the same volume. In a gas, like the air around us, atoms can move even faster and also change their distances, so the volume of the gas can increase or decrease.

➊ *There is movement even at the subatomic scale. Electrons spin and whirl around the nucleus of an atom. The proton and neutron particles in the nucleus vibrate or oscillate (move from side-to-side) slightly.*

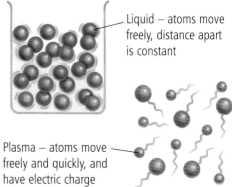

Liquid – atoms move freely, distance apart is constant

Plasma – atoms move freely and quickly, and have electric charge

World in **motion**

➊ *Gravity is the force of attraction that pulls everything in the Universe together. It acts on any object to pull it to the ground. The more mass an object has, the more the pull of gravity. A parachute or similar flat surface opens up to form a larger area for air to press against. Air resistance acts in the opposite direction to gravity and so slows the rate of fall back down to the ground.*

Amazing **facts**

• A force is measured in units called newtons (N).

• One newton of force will give an object of 1 kg an increase in speed of 1 m/sec.

• Pushing a car needs a force of about 500–1,000 N.

• The four jet engines of the retired airliner Concorde produced more than 700,000 N.

• When we measure the weight of an object, we measure the force of Earth's gravity pulling down on it. For example, a 100 g medium-sized apple is equivalent to about 1 N.

Are there different kinds of motion?

Yes, depending on the direction or path of the moving object. The simplest kind of motion is movement in a straight line, known as linear motion. Angular motion is in a bend or curve, such as a car going around a corner. A special case of this is circular motion, where the object stays the same distance from a central point, like a wheel on an axle.
Reciprocating motion is a to-and-fro movement from a middle point, such as pistons in an engine or the vibrations in a loudspeaker.

A nutcracker is a form of lever that provides the effort (squeezing force) to break the load (nut)

An axe is a form of wedge

A screw is a turning type of wedge

A wheelbarrow enables heavy loads to be lifted using a wheel and axle, which reduce friction to make the task easier

🔽 *As a motorcycle travels in a curved pathway, the rider must lean into the corner. This counteracts the natural tendency of a moving object to keep going in a straight line. Otherwise the motorcycle would topple outwards, away from the corner.*

What is a machine?

In basic science, a machine is a device that allows a small force, known as the effort, to move a large object, the load. There are six types of simple machine – the ramp (a slope or an inclined plane), lever, wedge, pulley, screw, and the wheel and axle. Examples of four of these are shown to the left. Of the remaining two machines, the ramp eases the movement of heavy objects over a distance. Pulleys move loads by changing the direction and distance of the force, to be pulled down, rather than lifted up. All other machines work by using various stages that are a combination of these simple machines.

Do machines give us extra energy?

No, it is not possible for machines to create energy or motion from nothing. As you pull out a nail with a crowbar, your hands move a long way without much force, while the other end of the lever moves a little way with a much greater force. This is known as mechanical advantage. It breaks a task down into smaller, easier stages so it becomes much more manageable. Many machines have motors or engines, which provide the force, rather than our own muscles, so the task becomes even easier.

Newton's **laws of motion**

➡ *Sir Isaac Newton (1642–1727) developed his ideas about gravity and motion in 1665–6. According to records, he began to form his theories after he saw an apple fall from a tree and wondered what force had pulled it to the ground.*

The laws

1 An object keeps moving in a straight line in the same direction (or keeps still if it's already still), unless a force acts on it.

2 A force makes an object change its movement in the direction of the force, with an acceleration (increase in speed) that depends on the size of the force.

3 For every action caused by a force, there is an equal and opposite reaction.

Examples

1 A spacecraft heading into outer space will keep going straight, unless it is affected by gravity from a planet or star, and pulled towards it.

2 Kick a football and it changes from being still to moving in the direction of the kick. Apply more force, which means a harder kick, and the ball gains speed faster and goes farther.

3 The engines of a jet-car blast hot gases backwards, which is the action. The reaction is to push the car forwards.

Many people wear wristwatches, and there are clocks in most rooms, which are there to tell us the time. We need to know the date and time so that we can arrive at school or work promptly, meet friends on agreed dates and at certain times, and in order to catch a bus, train or plane. However in science, there is much more to time than the tick of a clock.

⬆ *The ancient Egyptians made sundials more than 3,000 years ago. The marks showed hours. The length of the hours varied with the seasons, but people were used to such an idea and called them 'temporary hours'.*

When did people start measuring time?

At least 10,000 years ago, and probably well before that. Ancient peoples recorded sunrise and sunset each day, the changing phases of the moon each month, and the seasons of the year. They used these natural occurrences to devise calendars and predict important events, such as when a river might flood or the time to worship a certain god.

When were clocks first developed?

Ticking clocks similar to today's were devised in the 1300s. For centuries before, people had relied on simpler methods of timekeeping, such as hourglasses, or sundials. From the 1400s, however, explorers sailed on great voyages to find new lands. In order to track their positions, they needed to measure time precisely. In the 1700s, engineer John Harrison developed a series of very accurate clocks called chronometers (special clocks for use at sea to measure longitude). Accurate to less than 30 seconds in a year, even on a swaying ship, these began a new era of precise timekeeping.

Could time stand still?

Modern science predicts that yes, it might. We are used to time passing regularly, with every minute the same length, day after day, year after year. But Albert Einstein's theories said that time could change speed. The faster an object moves, the slower time passes. However, the speeds involved are enormous. If an object could move at the speed of light, then time might actually stop.

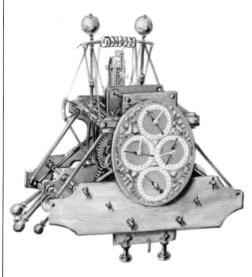

⬆ *John Harrison's 1759 version of the chronometer won a £10,000 prize. The prize had been devised by the British government in 1714 to promote research into the development of accurate timekeeping devices.*

⬅ *Simple timekeepers, such as hourglasses of trickling sand remained common until the 1300s when mechanical clocks were developed.*

Relativity

Albert Einstein

The theories of relativity developed by scientist Albert Einstein in 1905 and 1915 make some amazing predictions. From our everyday experience they seem to be impossible. But the predictions happen in extreme conditions out in the Universe, at incredible speeds and with vast objects such as stars and galaxies. In normal life here on Earth, the effects of Einstein's theories of relativity are so tiny that they can be measured, and they do not affect daily life. But out in the Universe, when travelling between the stars, the effects would be much more important. One effect is that as an object goes faster and faster, it shrinks in the direction that it is travelling.

⬆ *A rocket would get shorter lengthways, even though its width stays the same. To an observer on the outside, the rocket and the people in it would become shorter and fatter, and their clocks would become slower. To the people inside the rocket, everything seems normal within. But the Universe outside would look longer and thinner and clocks outside would tick much faster.*

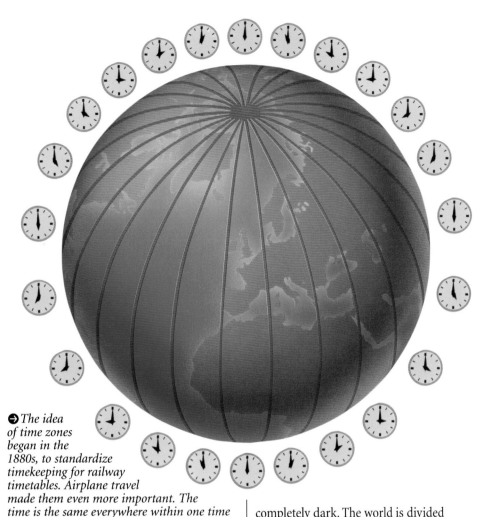

➡ *The idea of time zones began in the 1880s, to standardize timekeeping for railway timetables. Airplane travel made them even more important. The time is the same everywhere within one time zone, but different to all the other time zones.*

Is it the same time everywhere in the world?

No, because of the way the Earth spins around once every 24 hours. Otherwise at 8 a.m., the Sun might have risen in the UK, yet be setting in Australia, while the USA is completely dark. The world is divided into vertical strips called time zones. Some countries are within one time zone while others encompass several. Travellers need to adjust their watches or clocks as they move between zones to know the 'local' time. Some time zones 'bend' around islands or national borders.

Are time and space linked?

Yes, in modern science they are four parts or dimensions of the same whole. Three of these dimensions are in physical space – length, width and height. The fourth dimension is time. For example, to describe dangerous rocky rapids in a river, the length and width of the rapids, and the height that the water falls need to be measured. But the time of the measurement should also be recorded. Otherwise someone might arrive to see them in the dry season when the river and rapids have gone, and so the other measurements become irrelevant.

⬇ *Atomic clocks use the movement of atoms from substances such as caesium, which vibrate more than nine billion times each second, and are accurate to less than one second in a million years.*

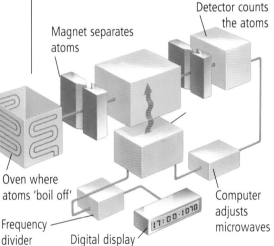

Detector counts the atoms
Magnet separates atoms
Oven where atoms 'boil off'
Frequency divider
Digital display
Computer adjusts microwaves

Amazing **facts**

• Time is relative. That is, it changes under different conditions, especially with speed of motion. The faster you move, the slower time passes.

• The only constant in the Universe, which is always the same, is the speed of light. This has the symbol c.

• Einstein showed that mass or matter, m, such as parts of atoms, could be changed into Energy, E.

• Einstein's famous equation was $E = mc^2$. This says that the amount of energy in a piece of mass, such as an atomic particle, equals the amount of mass times the speed of light multiplied by itself. Since light speed is huge, when multiplied by itself it is far greater. So a tiny bit of mass equals a vast amount of energy.

➡ *Albert Einstein (1879–1955) altered science greatly with his ideas about space and time. He showed they were relative – that is, they can change according to different conditions.*

Long ago, people travelled by foot and communicated face to face. It may have taken days to transport heavy goods just a few kilometres. Advances in transport and communication technology mean that we can now converse with a person on the other side of the world, using a videophone, or travel to be with that person within a day.

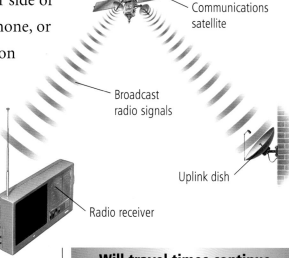

Communications satellite

Broadcast radio signals

Uplink dish

Radio receiver

➜ *Broadcast communications satellites send radio signals direct to many receivers over a wide area, for radio programmes and television channels.*

Is the world really 'shrinking'?

Planet Earth itself is not getting smaller. But a 'shrinking world' means we can travel and communicate much faster than previously. In the late 1700s, a journey halfway round the world by sailing ship might have taken three months. In the late 1800s, a similar journey by steamship took six weeks. In the 1920s, pioneering aeroplane flights over the same distance took just two weeks. Today the journey time halfway round the world has 'shrunk' to less than 24 hours.

Will travel times continue to shorten?

In the near future, probably not. There are various plans for 'space-planes' that could travel around the world in just a few hours. However, the costs of developing such a massive project are phenomenal. In the 1960s, many people thought that supersonic (faster-than-sound) aircraft travel would become widely-used. But the only supersonic passenger plane was Concorde, which first flew in the same year as the subsonic Boeing 747 'Jumbo'. Concorde could fly from Paris to Washington in a record time of 3 hrs 32 mins.

What is a comsat?

A communications satellite is designed to receive information such as radio programmes, telephone calls and television channels, usually sent to it in the form of 'uplink' radio waves. The satellite then strengthens or amplifies the signals and beams them back down again as radio waves. These satellites can be used as repeaters or relays to pass on information over great distances, or to broadcast to many receivers over a huge area. Most satellites are in geosynchronous orbits.

⬇ *The world is encircled by communications satellites and criss-crossed by telecom wires, fibre-optic cables, and radio and microwave links. The telecom network links telephone calls, radio, television and computer data.*

Inventions on the move

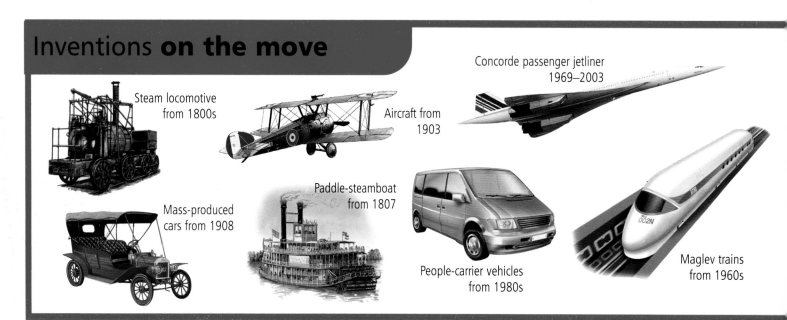

Steam locomotive from 1800s

Aircraft from 1903

Concorde passenger jetliner 1969–2003

Mass-produced cars from 1908

Paddle-steamboat from 1807

People-carrier vehicles from 1980s

Maglev trains from 1960s

→ *Present-day cruise ships are massive, and are organized much like floating hotels.*

What are the fastest forms of transport?

Rockets and spacecraft are the fastest, with the space shuttle travelling at more than 24,000 km/h. The fastest jet warplanes travel at more than 3,000 km/h, but a passenger jet plane moves at about 900 km/h. On land, electric-powered 'bullet trains' exceed 300 km/h. Passenger hovercraft on the sea reach 70–80 km/h and fast passenger ships around 40–50 km/h. Most cars reach up to 150 km/h but speed restrictions and crowded roads mean that journeys are often much slower and safer.

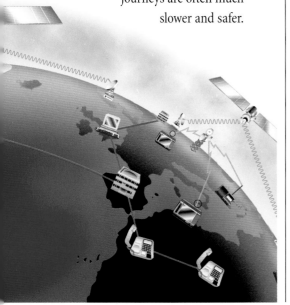

Will we have personal jump-jets or helicopters?

In the near future, probably not. There is only one working type of 'jump-jet' – the British Harrier multirole strike fighter. A newer US / British design, the JSF or Joint Strike Fighter, is taking years and costing billions to develop. Many important or wealthy people have personal helicopters. But the skills needed to fly a helicopter, and the strict limits on engineering, maintenance and safety mean that they are unlikely to become as common as cars in the near future.

Which form of travel is most luxurious?

Cruise liners offer amazing comfort and luxury, as 'floating hotels'. One of the biggest cruise liners is the *Queen Mary II*, which went into service in January 2004. It can carry 2,700 passengers at a top speed of 30 knots (equivalent to 55 km/h). The on-board facilities available to the passengers include 14 bars and clubs, six restaurants, a casino, theatre, swimming pools and even a planetarium.

↓ *'Jump-jets' such as the Harrier and JSF are VTOL – vertical take-off and landing aircraft. The jet blasts come out of tilting nozzles, which can point down for take-off and landing, or to the rear for forward flight.*

Amazing facts

GPS or satellite navigation

The Global Positioning System is a series of 24 NAVSTAR satellites circling Earth at an average height of 17,500 km. Of these satellites, 21 are active and three are spares.

Each satellite is about 5 m long and takes about 10 hours for each orbit.

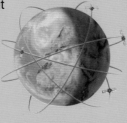

→ *GPS satellites continuously circle the Earth in groups.*

The satellites are in six groups, with four in each group that follow the same orbit one after the other.

At any time or place on the Earth, at least four satellites should be above the horizon, when their radio signals can be detected by a GPS receiver.

Each satellite's signals include its own identification and position, and the exact time from its on-board atomic clock.

The receiver works out the time delay for the signals from each satellite and compares them to find the receiver's location, usually to the nearest 20–30 m.

GEO for communications satellites

Many comsats are in GEO – geostationary or geosynchronous Earth orbit. In this position the satellite is 35,840 km above the Equator. It takes 24 hours to complete one orbit – which is the same time as the Earth beneath takes to spin around once.

So the satellite seems to 'hover' high in space above the same spot on the surface.

It means dishes sending and receiving signals can be aimed at the satellite and then left. They do not have to be continually adjusted to 'track' the satellite as it passes over.

Science and technology have filled our lives with machines, devices and gadgets. It seems incredible that just a few decades ago there were no CD players, satellite television or games consoles. Technical advances are moving at a tremendous rate with better and more efficient machines being constantly developed.

Detergent and additive trays

Controls

Drive belt

Motor

Door

Drum

Pump

Hydraulic suspension

Filter

How do CDs and DVDs store information?

CDs (compact discs) and DVDs (digital versatile discs) hold information in the form of tiny bowl-like pits in the shiny underside surface. In a CD there are over 3,000 million pits in a spiral path or track about 5 km long. They can store about 70 minutes of high-quality music, over 700 megabytes of computer data or similar amounts of information. A DVD has more, smaller pits in different vertical layers and stores 4.7 gigabytes (4,700 megabytes) – enough for a full-length movie and its soundtrack. These pits are 'read' by a laser beam.

◑ Personal music players can store sounds on tape, compact disc (like this version), minidisc (similar to CD but smaller) or electronic microchip.

◔ A powerful microscope reveals the bowl-like pits and flat areas between them, in the surface of a CD (compact disc).

◉ In western countries, such as the UK, about one household in two has a washing machine. About one in three households has a dishwasher.

Which labour-saving devices are most popular?

One of the most popular machines in daily life is the washing machine. In most developed countries, many households have one. Some people use industrial versions in launderettes. The machine washes clothes inside a revolving drum with hot water and soap, which are then rinsed away with clean water. A fast spin gets rid of excess water, so that the clothes can be hung to dry.

Technical developments

Key dates

The second half of the 20th century saw an explosion in technology:

1950	First commercials or 'adverts' shown on colour television.
1953	Heart-lung machines in medicine.
1955	Development of optical fibres.
1958	Ultrasound scans check babies in the womb.
1959	Photocopiers are first sold commercially.
1960	First laser developed.
1961	Live television by satellite.
1963	Audio cassette introduced.
1965	Development of holograms.
1967	UK begins colour television broadcasts.
1969	First Moon landing.
1970	Removable floppy discs for computers.
1972	Early home computer games with tennis-like bats and ball.

◉ Holograms show 3-D images, with depth as well as width and height, on a flat surface.

Can mobile phones get much smaller?

The main limits on mobile phone size are the rechargeable battery bulk and the size of the buttons so they are easy for our fingers to press. Also, screens for photos and videos cannot be too small. In the future mobile phones may become voice-operated so that they do not need buttons. For security it will only respond to the unique voice of its owner.

◄ Mobile phones have shrunk amazingly in the past 10 years, from the size of a housebrick to almost as small as a thumb.

Does medicine benefit from technology?

Yes, technology is very important in many aspects of modern medicine. For example, an endoscope is a flexible tube that can be inserted into the body to view its insides to achieve a more detailed and accurate diagnosis. Light to illuminate the interior is carried to the tip along optical fibres, which are bundled, flexible rods of transparent glass or plastic, thinner than human hairs. The image is carried from the tip to the eyepiece and screen by another set of optical fibres. There are also many kinds of scanners that can see inside the body.

◑ Doctors can see inside the body using various kinds of scanners, or directly by looking through an endoscope. The endoscope can also carry out treatments, such as sealing a cut using a laser beam.

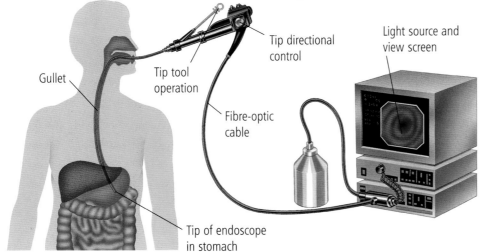

Gullet

Tip tool operation

Tip directional control

Fibre-optic cable

Light source and view screen

Tip of endoscope in stomach

Main unit feeds images to monitor or television

Hand console with controls

↑ Games consoles become more realistic every year, with faster action and better graphics, as well as more imaginative challenges. Some games can be played 'live' over the Internet with people anywhere in the world.

How fast does technology become out-of-date?

Technology is frequently updated, making existing versions out-of-date. For example, vinyl discs were used to play back recorded sound for more than 50 years. Cassette tapes also became popular for about 30 years. About 20 years later, CDs took over. Some 10 years after that, MP3-players arrived, storing sounds in electronic microchips. The world of technology continues to produce faster and more efficient machines.

1975	First commercial 'flat screen' LCDs, liquid crystal displays.
1977	Mass-produced pocket televisions.
1979	Personal music players (audio cassette).
1981	First PCs (personal computers) as we now recognize them.
1982	Audio CDs, compact discs, go on sale.
1984	Camcorders developed.
1987	DAT, digital audio tape.
1988	Colour laser photocopiers; early mobile phones.
1989	'Gameboy' early hand-held games console.
1990	Bag-less vacuum cleaners.
1992	Superbike cycles with many composite materials.
1993	Early videophones.
1994	Internet users exceed 30 million.
1995	A standard format for the DVD is agreed.
1996	'Playstation 1' games.
1998	Apple introduces iMac computers.
1999	International Space Station construction under way, bringing the idea of 'holidays in space'.
2000	DVDs begin to sell in commercial quantities.

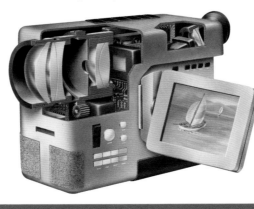

◄ The camcorder is a personal movie camera and videotape recorder. Some models can now fit in the palm of the hand.

Why not test your knowledge on science and technology! Try answering these questions to find out how much you know about electronics, chemicals and compounds, heat, motion, atoms, radioactivity and much more. Questions are grouped into the subject areas covered within the pages of this book. See how much you remember and discover how much more you can learn.

14 Which musical invention was first called a phonograph?

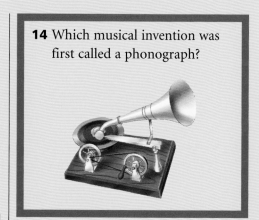

The Basics of Matter

1 What does water become when it boils?
2 Iron, steel and copper are examples of what?
3 What happens to water at 0°C?

Chemicals and Compounds

4 What happens to butter when it is heated?
5 What is solid water called?
6 Which natural liquid is used to make nylon?

Structures and Materials

8 What supports a building?
9 Which will feel hotter after stirring a hot drink: a plastic or metal spoon?
10 What is used to attach a door to its frame but lets it open and close?

Energy and Work

11 Which tool is used to push in and pull out nails?
12 What gives your body energy?
13 What is the name for a machine made of ropes and wheels used to lift heavy loads?

Electricity and Power

15 What is an example of natural electricity?
16 What does 'AC' stand for in electrical matters?
17 Does a conductor let energy flow, or stop it flowing?

Magnetism

18 A magnet has an east and west pole: true or false?
19 What is special about a compass needle?
20 What navigational device uses a magnet suspended or floating in liquid?

The Electronic Age

21 In what kind of station is electricity made?
22 What is used to make electricity in a hydro-electric power station?
23 What did Thomas Edison invent to create light in 1879?

7 Pierre and Marie Curie, who worked together to investigate radioactivity, shared which prize in 1903 with Henri Becquerel, who discovered radioactivity?

Rays and Radiation

24 What are the straight lines that light travels in called?

25 What type of rays are used to take a photograph of your bones?

26 Which type of radiation can cause sunburn or skin cancer?

Light and Lasers

27 What is the curved glass in spectacles called?

28 The seven colours of the spectrum combine to make what colour light?

29 Light bends when it goes through water: true or false?

Sound

30 Which word describes how loud sound is?

31 How do you make a sound on a percussion instrument?

32 Do the thick or thin strings on a guitar sound lowest?

33 Who developed the first hot-air balloon, launched in 1783?

Force, Motion and Machines

34 What has sails that turn round in the wind to work machinery?

35 Which English scientist developed the first modern theory about how gravity works?

36 What is kinetic energy?

Time and Space

37 Could we live on any other planet apart from Earth?

38 How many hours are there in a day?

39 Length, breadth and width are three dimensions: what is the fourth?

Transport and Communications

40 What kind of boat floats on air?

41 What is the name for the strip where an aircraft lands?

42 What did Alexander Graham Bell invent in 1876?

Technology Today and Tomorrow

43 What do radios and televisions have for picking up signals?

44 Does a computer programmer develop hardware or software?

45 What is used to receive signals from a satellite?

Answers

1 Steam	13 Pulley	24 Rays	36 Movement energy
2 Metals	14 Gramophone	25 X-rays	37 No
3 It freezes	15 Lightning	26 Ultra-violet rays	38 24
4 It melts	16 Alternating current	27 A lens	39 Time
5 Ice	17 It lets it flow	28 White light	40 Hovercraft
6 Oil	18 False – it has a North	29 True	41 Runway
7 Nobel Prize for Physics	and a South pole	30 Volume	42 The telephone
8 Foundations	19 It is a magnet	31 You bang or rattle it	43 Aerials
9 Metal spoon	20 Magnetic compass	32 The thick strings	44 Software
10 Hinge	21 In a power station	33 The Montgolfier brothers	45 Satellite dish
11 Hammer	22 Water	34 A windmill or wind turbines	
12 Food	23 The light bulb	35 Sir Isaac Newton	

Page numbers in **bold** refer to main subjects; page numbers in *italics* refer to illustrations.

A

acetone 11, *11*
acoustics **26–27**, *26, 27*
air 10
air pressure 26
aircraft 13, 26, 28, 32, *32*, 33, *33*
  B-2 stealth bomber 26, *26*
  Boeing 747 'Jumbo' 33
  Harrier jump jet 33, *33*
  helicopters 33
  JSF (Joint Strike Fighter) 33
  Mach speed 26
  military 26, *26*, 33, *33*
  supersonic *32*
alpha particles 22, *22*, 23
alpha radiation 22
alternating current (AC) 17
aluminium 13, 18
amps (amperes) 17, 20
asphalts 11
atomic clocks 31, *31*
atoms 8, *8*, 9, 10, *10*, 11, 12, 15, *15*, 16
  bombs 10, 11, *11*, 27, *27*
  electricity 16, 17, *17*
  laser light 24, *24*
  magnetism 18
  motion 28, *28*, 29, *29*
axles 29

B

B-2 stealth bomber 26, *26*
batteries 17, *17*
beta particles 22, *22*, 23
bitumens 11
Bohr, Neils 10, 11, *11*
Boyle, Robert 8
buildings 12
bullet-proof vests 13, *13*
butane 11

C

cables 16, 17, 33
calories 15
camcorders 35, *35*
cans 13, 18
capacitors 21
carbon 9, *9*, 11, *11*
carbon fibre 13

cars 12, 13, *13*, 20, 26, 28, 29, 32, 33
cathode rays 10
CDs (compact discs) 34, *34*, 35
ceramics 12, 16
Chadwick, James 10
chemical elements 8, 9, *9*, 10, 11
chemicals **10–11**, *10, 11*, 17
chlorine 9, *9*
chronometers 30, *30*
clocks 30, 31, *31*
coal 15, *15*
colour 24, 25, *24–25*
communications **32–33**, *32–33*
  satellites 32, 33, *32–33*
compasses 18, 19, *19*
composites 13
compounds **10–11**, *10, 11*
computers 16, 20, *20*, 34, 35
  games consoles 34, 35, *35*
  music recording 34, 35
Concorde 28, 32, *32*
conductors 12, *12*, 13, 16, *16*
copper 12, *12*
covalent bonds 10, *10*
CPUs (central processing units) 21
cranes 28
crystals 13
cycles (bicycles) 28, 35

D

Dalton, John 8, 9, *9*
decibel scale 27, *27*
Democritus 8
dimensions 31
diodes 21
direct current (DC) 17
DVDs (Digital Versatile Discs) 34, 35

E

e-mail 26
Earth 8, 10, 14, 22, 28
  communications network 32–33, *32–33*
  magnetism 18–19, *18, 19*
  time 30–31, *30, 31*
earthquakes 15
echo 27
  echolocation 26, *26*, 27, *27*
Einstein, Albert 30–31, *30, 31*
electricity 10, 12, 13, **16–17**, *16, 17*
  appliances 12, 16, 34–35, *34, 35*
  electronics 20–21, *20, 21*

electricity *(continued)*
  motors 19, *19*
  static 16, *16*
electromagnetism 19, *19*, 20, 22, 23
  light 24, 25
  radiation 22, *22*
electronics **20–21**, *20, 21*
electrons 8, *8*, 10, *10*, 16, 17, 18
  motion 28, *28*, 29
  television 20, *20*
elements 8, 9, *9*, 10, 11
EM spectrum 23
endoscopes 35, *35*
energy **14–15**, *14, 15*
  Einstein, Albert 31, *31*
  light 24
  machines 29
  sound 26, 27
engines 26, 29
ethane 11

F

Fermi, Enrico 10
Fleming, Ambrose 20
force **28–29**, *28, 29*
frequencies 22
fuels 11, 15, 17

G

games consoles 34, 35, *35*
gamma rays 22, *22*, 23
gas (fuel) 15, 17
gases 8, 9, 11
  atoms 28, *28*, 29
GEO (geosynchronous Earth orbit) 32, 33
glass 10, 12, *12*, 16, 27
glass-reinforced plastic (GRP) 13
GPS (Global Positioning System) 33
gravity 28, 29

H

Harrier jump jet 33, *33*
Harrison, John 30
heat 12, 14, 16, 17
helicopters 33
helium 8, *8*, 22
holograms 34, *34*
hydrocarbons (CHs) 11
hydroelectric power 17
hydrogen 8, *8*, 11

I

inclined plane 29
infra-red 22, *22*, 23, 24
insulators 12, 16
integrated circuits 21, *21*
International Space Station 35
Internet 35
ionic bonds 10, *10*
iron 13, *13*, 18

J

jets *see* aircraft

K

kerosene 11
Kilby, Jack 20

L

laser light **24–25**, *24–25*, 34
Lavoisier, Antoine, 8, 9, *9*
LCDs (liquid crystal displays) 35
levers 29, *29*
light 14, 16, 22, **24–25**, *24–25*, 27
  bulbs 15, 16, 17
  speed of 23, 25
lightning 15
liquids 28, *28*, 29
lodestone (magnetite) 18, *18*
loudspeakers 19, *19*, 26

M

Mach
  scale 26, *26*
  speed 26
Mach, Ernst 26
machines
  axles 29
  levers 29, *29*
  ramps 29
  screws 29
magnetism **18–19**, *18*, *19*
materials **12–13**, *12*, *13*
matter **8–9**, *8*, *9*
measuring electricity 16, *16*, 17
  energy 15
  force 28
  strength 12
  time 30–31, *30*, *31*
mechanics **28–29**, *28*, *29*
  mechanical advantage 29
medical technology 34, 35, *35*

endoscopes 35, *35*
Mendeleév, Dmitri 8
metals 8, 10, 12, 13, 16, 18
  processing 13, *13*
methane (marsh gas) 11
microchips 20, 21, *21*
microprocessors *see* CPUs
microwaves 22, *22*, 23, *23*, 24, 32
minerals 13, 22
mirrors 24, *24*, 27
molecules 10, *10*, 11, *11*, 12
monomers 12
Moon landings 34
Moore, Gordon (Moore's Law) 21
motion 14, 16, 23, **28–29**, *28*, *29*
motorcycles 28, *28*, 29, *29*
motors 26, 29
  electric 19, *19*
movement *see* motion
multimeters 16, *16*

N

nanometres 9, 25
natural materials 12
neutrons 8, *8*, 9, 10, 15, *15*, 22
  motion 28, *28*, 29, *29*
Newton, Sir Isaac 29, *29*
Newton's laws 29, *29*
newtons 28
North Pole 18, 19
nuclear
  force 9
  physics 10, 11, *10*, *11*
  power 15, *15*, 23, *23*
nucleus 8, *8*, 9, 10, 15, *15*, 18, 28, *28*, 29, *29*

O

ohms 17
oil 15, 17
  refineries 11, *11*
optical fibres 34, 35, *35*
oxygen 8, *8*, 9, 10, 11, *11*

P

particles
  alpha 22, *22*, 23
  beta 22, *22*, 23
PCBs (printed circuitboards) 21, *21*
Periodic Table 8, 9, *9*
petrol 11
photocopiers 34, 35

photons 24
photovoltaic cells 21
planes *see* aircraft
plasma 28, *28*
plastic 10, 11, 12, 13, 16, 18, 27
plutonium 23
poles, magnetic 18
polyethylene (Polythene) 12
polymers 12
polystyrene 12
polyurethane 12
power **16–17**, *16*, *17*
power stations 14, *14*, 15, 17, *17*
  hydro-electric 17
  nuclear 23, *23*
propane 11
protons 8, *8*, 9, 22
  motion 29, *29*
pulleys 29

Q

quantum theory 11
quarks 8
Queen Mary II 33

R

radar 22, *22*
radiation **22–23**, *22*, *23*
radio 16, 22, *22*, 24, 32, 33
radioactive decay 22, *22*
radium 23
ramps 29
rays 14, **22–23**, *22*, *23*
refraction 25, *25*
relativity 30, 31
resistors 21
Rutherford, Ernest 10, 11, *11*

S

satellites **32–33**, *32*, *33*, 34
scanners 34, 35
screws 29
shells (atoms) 9, *9*, 10
ships 13, 30, 32, *32*
  cruise liners 33
Shockley, William 20
silicon 21
silver 12, 16
sodium 9, *9*
sodium chloride (salt) 10, *10*, 11
soil 10
solids 28, *28*, 29

sonic boom 26
sonic clicks 27, *27*
sound 14, 16, **26–27**, *26, 27*
South Pole 18, 19
space 23, 25, **30–31**, *30, 31*
spacecraft 15, *15*, 29
   International Space Station 35
   rockets 12, *12*, 30, *30*
   shuttle 33
spectra **22–23**
   visible light spectrum 24, 25, *24, 25*
speed of
   light 23, 25
   sound 26, 27
   time 30, 31
   transport 32, 33
static electricity 16, *16*
steam 17, 32
steel 13, 18, 27
strings (string theory) 8
structures **12–13**, *12, 13*
subatomic particles 8, *8*, 9, 23
submarines 15
Sun 8, 15
   radiation 22, *22*
sundials 30, *30*
supersonic aircraft 32, *32*

T

technological developments **34–35**, *34–35*
telecommunications **32–33**, *32, 33*
telephones 16, 20, 32, 33, 35, *35*

television 12, 16, 20, *20*, 22, 26, 32, 34
Thomson, J. J. 10
time 25, *25*, **30–31**, *30, 31*
tin 13
tools 12
trains 26, 33
   maglev 18, *18*, 32, *32*
transformers 17, *17*, 21
transistors 21
transport **32–33**, *32, 33*
turbines 14, *14*, 17

U

ultra-violet 22, *22*, 23, 24
ultrasonic sound 26
ultrasound scans 34
Universe 8, 14, 23, 30, 31
uranium 8, *8*, 23

V

vacuum cleaners 28, 35
vibrations 26
volts 17, 20

W

washing machines 20, 34, *34*
water 10, 17,
   plumbing 26
   sound 27
waterwheels 15, *15*

watts 17
waves 22, 24
weather 9
wedges 29
wheels 29
wind turbines 14, *14*, 17
wires 12, *12*, 13, 16, 33
wood 10, 11, 12, 16, 18, 29
work (energy) **14–15**, *14, 15*
wormholes 25, *25*
wristwatches 30, 31

X

X-rays 22, *22*, 23, 24

Z

Zworykin, Vladimir 20

The publishers would like to thank the following artists who have contributed to this book:
John Butler, Kuo Kang Chen, Mark Davis, Peter Dennis, Nicholas Forder, Shammi Ghale, Peter Gregory, Alan Hancocks, Peter Harper, Rob Jakeway, Maltings, Janos Marffy, Martin Sanders, Peter Sarson, Mike Saunders, Guy Smith, Rudi Vizi, Mike White, Paul Williams, John Woodcock

The publishers wish to thank the following for the photographs used in this book:
Robert Essel NYC/CORBIS p16 (c/r); Apple Computers p20 (b/l); Richard T. Nowitz/CORBIS p21 (t/r); Sony Computer Entertainment p21(b/c); SAM YEH/AFP/GETTY IMAGES p27 (c/r); AFP/GETTY IMAGES p32 (c/l); FRANK PERRY/AFP/GETTY IMAGES p33 (t/r); Sony Computer Entertainment p35 (t/r)

All other photographs are from:
Corel, Digital Vision, digitalSTOCK, ILN, PhotoDisc